BUILD

—

**ELEMENTS OF AN
EFFECTIVE SOFTWARE
ORGANIZATION**

Copyright © 2024 Swarmia. All rights reserved.

ISBN-13: 979-8-218-32190-1

Book version: 2.0—January 2024

Contents

Preface	vi
1 INTRODUCTION	**3**
How we approach effectiveness in this book	4
How we talk about teams	6
Setting the stage for an effectiveness effort	7
Measurement and goal-setting	10
A note on frameworks	14
Table stakes	14
What we left out	17
What to expect from this book	19
2 BUSINESS OUTCOMES	**20**
Organizing for outcomes	21
Balancing engineering investments	38
What to do when you're drowning in KTLO	43
Setting priorities	45
OKRs: A framework to communicate priorities	47
Managing cross-team initiatives	52
3 DEVELOPER PRODUCTIVITY	**58**
Defining developer productivity	59
Measuring productivity	68
Classic productivity challenges	77
Setting goals around productivity	78
Tools and tactics	80

4 DEVELOPER EXPERIENCE — 84

- Measuring developer experience — 85
- Identifying improvements — 86
- Fighting back against interruptions — 93
- Setting experience goals — 105

5 PUTTING IT ALL TOGETHER — 110

- Identifying and eliminating delivery bottlenecks — 111
- Driving an effectiveness effort — 119
- Managing change — 124
- What's next? — 128

- About the authors — 131
- About Swarmia — 131
- Acknowledgments — 132
- Feedback and errata — 132

Preface

by **Otto Hilska**
Founder & CEO of Swarmia

Engineering organizations are operating in unfamiliar territory. Not so long ago, hiring more engineers was the obvious solution to increase output and drive growth. Many engineering leaders fell into the trap of believing that the sheer increase in numbers would lead to getting more done.

Looking back, this never truly made sense. We've known since *The Mythical Man-Month* that adding people — especially if you do so quickly — is actually a recipe for slowing down, yet it was a path well-worn by countless companies.

Now the landscape has changed, and sometimes it feels like it happened overnight. Suddenly, there's abundant uncertainty about how to deliver more business outcomes with fixed-size teams. Moreover, no company wants to do it in a way that strains the engineers doing the work. In fact, the most positive changes can occur with systematic approaches that make individual engineers more productive by improving the experience of building software in your organization.

Leaders are responsible for building the framework that allows teams and individuals to succeed in this new environment. It's no longer about throwing more bodies into the fray and hoping everything works out. Today, it's about implementing transparency, defining supportive processes, and driving coherent strategies that align the goals and incentives of the software engineers, their teams, and the products they build.

This book exists to help you navigate that space. There's a never-ending stream of guidance out there about each of these topics — developer experience, developer productivity, and driving business outcomes — but very few resources that bring all of them together under a single umbrella. This book attempts to close that gap.

The systems and ecosystems we build to help us deliver software products are fundamentally human, and no organization is exactly like another. Whether you're at the outset of a journey to hone the value created by your software development organization or you're already somewhere along the way, finding the best path to success starts by understanding the unique context of your company.

To that end, this book is not a mere collection of recommendations; it's a guide to understanding the bigger picture of engineering effectiveness, including hard-earned wisdom about the inevitable pitfalls and dead-end paths that may tempt you along the way.

If you find this topic as interesting as I do, this book is for you. Happy reading.

Build

⭐

**Elements of an
Effective Software
Organization**

By Rebecca Murphey & Otto Hilska

Build: Elements of an Effective Software Organization

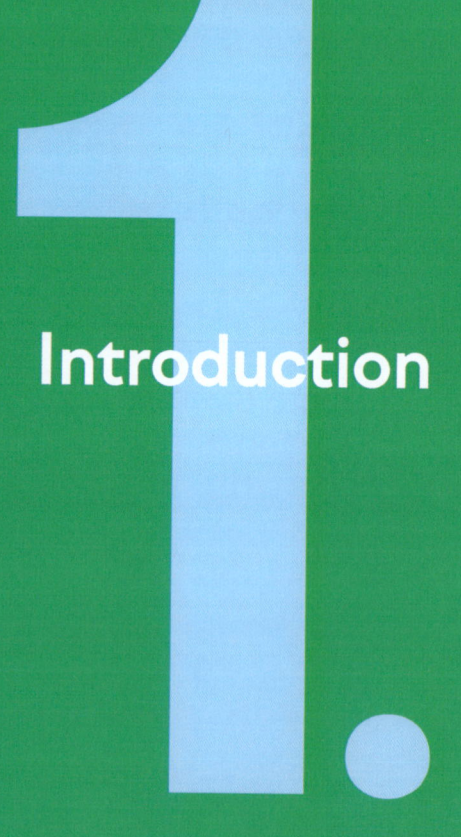

Introduction

1.

There are plenty of origin stories for a company's decision to invest in sustaining and improving the effectiveness of its engineering organization. Sometimes it's a simple conversation among leaders: "Is it just me, or did we ship things faster in the past?" Sometimes it's preceded by painful failure: "We missed most of our objectives last half, and product and engineering are pointing fingers at each other." And sometimes, it's driven more by curiosity about an opportunity than an acute or targeted need: "I've heard of SPACE and DORA, and I think they could help us."

Each of these origin stories — and every other story that eventually leads a person like you to read a book like this — has a unique motivation. How the problem is stated tells you much about the underlying issues you'll find when you dig into the situation. It's relatively easy to adopt a new approach when you can operate with curiosity and a mindset of continuous improvement, but it's much more challenging when you're trying to solve an acute problem within the constraints of a company's current size, age, and culture.

> **How the problem is stated tells you much about the underlying issues you'll find when you dig into the situation.**

This book aims to collect the best practices of software product development, drawing on lean principles, modern product and project management principles, systems thinking, and much more. Much has been written on these individual

THE EFFECTIVENESS TRIAD

- BUSINESS OUTCOMES
- DEVELOPER PRODUCTIVITY
- DEVELOPER EXPERIENCE

topics across various books — see our recommended reading at the end of each of the following chapters — but here, we attempt to pull it all together into a coherent framework for running a software organization.

How we approach effectiveness

We like to think of effectiveness by breaking it down into three concepts: ❶ **business outcomes**, ❷ **developer productivity**, and ❸ **developer experience**. Delivering business outcomes is the ultimate goal of any software organization. Once you know where you're headed, developer productivity is about getting there quickly. Developer experience is about discovering how you might increase the continuous time an engineer can focus on valuable work while remaining satisfied and engaged with their job.

Many discussions of engineering effectiveness focus on just one of these concepts without recognizing that they are all intertwined. In this book, we look at each area individually and then discuss how to bring them together into a coherent and actionable plan for improvement.

> **Many discussions of engineering effectiveness focus on just one of these concepts without recognizing that they are all intertwined.**

① BUSINESS OUTCOMES

A fundamental challenge of delivering a successful product is intelligently allocating finite resources to seemingly infinite problems and opportunities. The decisions involved here are difficult at any organization size, and they aren't limited to software engineering. Organizational design plays a huge role in how well a business can achieve its goals. There's a real risk of trying to do too many things at once, with the inevitable result that few of them get done well, if at all. In larger organizations, these decisions often happen organically and implicitly, with fuzzy lines of accountability and no clear overarching picture of who's spending time (and money) on what.

> **Effective software organizations focus their investments on the right outcomes.**

② DEVELOPER PRODUCTIVITY

Without intention and intervention, the pace of shipping value will decline over time, and doing what has always worked won't always keep working. Engineering leaders are increasingly held accountable for the value their organizations deliver — and they are increasingly at risk of people outside engineering deciding how to quantify this value. The processes that move work through an engineering organization — ideally creating customer value at the end — are evolving, emergent, and often difficult to inspect or understand. As an organization grows larger, the leverage points to drive improvement move from the team to the organization as a whole, and the forces that speed or impede delivery become more varied and broadly distributed.

> **Effective software organizations make fast and consistent progress toward their goals.**

③ DEVELOPER EXPERIENCE

Developer experience is arguably the other side of the developer productivity coin, and it can be hard to separate the two. Developer experience focuses on what it's like to work within your organization's code and deliver its software. Developer experience efforts should emphasize eliminating wait time and interruptions, ensuring that your codebase isn't making work harder than it needs to be.

> **Effective software organizations give engineers the support and tools they need to feel engaged.**

How we talk about teams

Throughout the book, we use a few words consistently to describe the scope of a situation, problem, or solution.

- **The business.** The overarching entity that pays the bills. It encompasses the engineering organization as well as other functions such as sales, marketing, customer support, finance, and more.

- **The organization or the engineering organization.** The group of people responsible for delivering technical solutions to achieve business objectives, including software engineers, product managers, product designers, and other supporting roles.

- **The group.** A group of related engineering teams, usually led by a director, that's part of a larger engineering organization.

- **The team.** A cross-functional group of people focused on delivering technical solutions to specific business problems, usually in the context of a specific problem, product, or persona.

Setting the stage for an effectiveness effort

If creating an effective software organization is A Thing You Should Care About in your role — whether you're a line manager or the CTO — it's good to ask yourself a few questions to prepare for the conversation ahead.

- **Why is this important?** What's motivating the company to spend time on this topic? How does it beat out other goals? How high up does the plan go?

- **Why is this important now?** Software organizations can always be more effective, but now is suddenly the time you're paying attention. What changed?

- **What have you tried so far?** How did you decide you needed to do something else?

- **What metrics are you tracking today?** Where are they falling short? How are they changing over time?

Smaller companies may still need to nail the delivery fundamentals at the team level, while larger companies may form dedicated teams to standardize, automate, and speed up development processes. At a certain size, it takes effort just to sustain the same amount of productivity; even if the engineering headcount isn't growing, the codebase is, and quickly. As a company grows, its investment in its continued effectiveness needs to grow too, as the later that investment starts, the more debt must be paid down. At a certain size, you'll consider a dedicated platform team to keep that software development ecosystem humming as you continually accumulate lines of code.

CHALLENGES INCREASE OVER TIME

Credit: John Cutler

A company's culture determines the likely pace, breadth, and "stickiness" of its improvements. Companies that highly value team technical autonomy face different challenges than companies with standardized tooling and centralized processes. The depth of trust throughout the leadership chain will influence how readily people embrace productivity efforts, and the company's engineering ladder will play a big part in who raises their hand to do the work. When thinking about how to drive change, don't pick fights with the culture. Instead, use it to your advantage whenever you can and reshape it (gently) only when you must.

Answering the following questions will deepen your understanding of how these three factors come into play.

- **What does "better" look like?** Your engineering effectiveness investment proposal was approved. It's two years later, and everything is better. You can't believe you used to spend time doing … what? What has changed? Looking at the current reality, what's kept you from making these changes?

- **Who benefits when we achieve better?** This is a trick question because the answer is "everyone," from product to sales, customer support to engineering to users. Where will you find reliable allies and champions for more effective delivery — even if it comes at some near-term costs such as slower delivery of bug fixes and new features?

- **What kinds of potential changes are in scope?** Does the business think of this as an engineering problem, a business problem, or both? What is the scope of the most senior person who will sponsor necessary change, even if it has near-term costs? Who will warm up to the cause after a couple of success stories?

- **What are the biggest obstacles you expect?** Now is not the time for rosy optimism. Talk openly with anyone who wants to pitch in about what will be hard. Maybe two different engineering organizations aren't aligned on what's important; maybe you expect the CEO to defer to product priorities instead. Maybe everyone's on the same page but you worry that procuring a tool will take six months. This sort of effort can go sideways in many regards, so anticipate whatever you can.

Each company takes its own path to arrive at the start of its productivity journey, and the path it follows after that will likewise be unique. There is plenty to learn from what others are doing, plenty we can standardize as an industry, and plenty you can discover from this book.

Anyone who tells you there's One True Way is lying. The way to improve your situation will be unique to the size, age, and culture of the company in which you operate.

Measurement and goal-setting

Being a software leader would be a lot easier if we didn't have to figure out whether we were doing a good job. Of course, every data-driven bone in our bodies says we need to measure something to know we're going in the right direction, and every company leader would likely agree.

We'll delve into specific measurements in the upcoming chapters, but a few caveats generally apply to measuring things in this space.

First, it's easy to get bogged down in figuring out how to measure the impact of something rather than doing The Thing. With enough time and code, you'll probably get there, but remember to ask yourself whether that time is worth the benefit. Sometimes, all you need to do is ① make sure no one thinks The Thing is a terrible idea, ② do The Thing, and ③ check in with your users or stakeholders to see whether they noticed that you did The Thing. Don't fall into the trap of delaying action — and thereby delaying benefit — just because you haven't yet worked out how you'll count something. Be prepared to advocate for and celebrate clear-if-unmeasurable wins.

Second, metrics — especially qualitative ones — can be difficult to interpret correctly and consistently. The space is full of both lagging indicators of success and indicators that can be hard to trust because they're biased by a moment in time. Self-reported satisfaction scores, for example, are deeply subject to moment-in-time bias, even to the whims of traffic on the commute to work that day. They can drop quickly and tend to recover slowly. Decisions on how you slice your data can also hide problems. An average metric might overemphasize outliers, while p50 can hide pathological cases at p99. On the other hand, looking at p99 all the time can lead to optimizations that benefit relatively few use cases.

Third, there's a fine balance between metrics that guide improvements and those that make people perceive a lack of trust. However, this tension shouldn't stop you from measuring. Instead, it emphasizes the need to be open and transparent about the data you collect, how you collect it, and how you use it to evaluate individuals and teams. Be transparent with individual contributors (ICs) about what you're measuring and how it will be used. Make it easy for them to see the data they're contributing.

Finally, remember that these kinds of metrics work best as conversation starters and pretty terribly as comparison metrics when there's a change in context — for example, a staffing change or a change in priorities. The conversations the metrics drive will differ from team to team — teams tend to have meaningful differences in their skill sets, tenure, seniority, codebases, complexity, and so much more that it becomes irresponsible to compare them head to head.

> **There's a fine balance between metrics that guide improvements and those that make people perceive a lack of trust.**

With these caveats in mind, you can see how goal-setting around any metric in the effectiveness domain will likely have some gotchas. Be especially wary of setting goals around human-reported metrics — for example, a developer satisfaction metric or one that counts how often engineers complain about something.

Choosing metrics and tracking progress

The desire for measurement can paralyze an effectiveness effort. Metrics are valuable, but a lack of them shouldn't block progress on well-known problems.

Decisions on how and whether to measure something should be the output of a thoughtful and deliberative process about what better would look like. It's okay if some of your ambitions are intangible, such as "Deploy issues shouldn't dominate our next developer survey."

The Goals, Signals, and Metrics framework is helpful here — and note that metrics come last.

- **Goals** focus on outcomes, not the anticipated implementation.
- **Signals** are things that humans can watch for to know if you're on track.
- **Metrics** are the actual things you measure and report on to track progress toward the goal.

In this framework, you first agree that there's a problem worth solving. Then, you set a goal that, if achieved, would be clearly understood as progress toward solving the problem. Next, you have the "I know it when I see it" conversation — what statements, if true, would have everyone nodding in agreement that you were progressing? These are your signals.

Finally, you arrive at the metrics, but again, a word of caution: don't beat yourself up to measure something when broad agreement about the existence of a clear signal would be sufficient to declare success, nor when the change has another, more notable business impact. There's a ton of accruing value to measuring your development process, but not all aspects of productivity can be measured conveniently, if at all.

Working on a goal often starts by establishing a baseline for the current reality. Stay focused on the desired outcome, not the metric or tactic. Keep your focus on making things easier for engineers, use that focus to motivate increased observability of processes, execute on the opportunities you find, and know that quantitative data will sometimes disagree with the stories you've been told.

You may initially find it difficult to set a specific target for the metrics, and that's not just okay but expected. When tackling a problem, focus on trends — up or down and to the right as appropriate. If you continue to focus on the issue over subsequent quarters, you'll have more information to set targets or acceptable thresholds.

A note on frameworks

There are numerous frameworks to help you improve your software organization — SPACE and DORA are a couple that are currently in fashion. Each framework is useful in its own way, and they're all worth knowing about, but none tell you what to do in your particular situation. None of them can claim to offer a single metric that you can observe and set goals around — in fact, only DORA is particularly prescriptive about any metrics at all.

If you approach the productivity space with a mindset of "I need to implement DORA" or "We'll just follow SPACE," you'll likely have difficulty driving meaningful change. Frameworks offer a way of thinking about a problem, not a to-do list. They're a skeleton on which you hang some ideas that will turn into a plan, which you'll then implement and iterate upon.

A framework can also offer guardrails against counterproductive decisions if stakeholders agree to it on principle. For example, a core tenet of SPACE is that metrics that span the framework can often be in tension with one another. This tenet can be a good reminder when metrics aren't moving the way you might have expected.

Table stakes

Any effectiveness effort becomes significantly easier if you adopt and embrace a few proven principles. These principles are so essential that we'll revisit them throughout the rest of this book, whose guidance will be of limited use if you don't also embrace or move toward these principles in your organization. Indeed, if your engineering organization struggles to be effective, at least one of these principles is probably absent.

1. **Empowered teams.** When teams can make autonomous decisions about their work, organizations can respond more quickly to changes, improve motivation, and ship solutions more likely to meet customer needs. When they must rely on others to make progress, the effectiveness of their teams suffers.

2. **Rapid feedback.** Quick and frequent feedback enables rapid learning and adjustments. This agility helps better align the product with market needs and customer expectations. When you have weeks-long feedback cycles, a lot can go wrong between check-ins.

3. **Outcomes over outputs.** Focus on the value and impact (outcomes) of engineering work rather than just the volume or efficiency of deliverables produced (outputs). This ensures that development efforts actually contribute to business goals and customer value.

Let's dig into each of these in more detail to see what they look like in practice.

1 EMPOWERED TEAMS

Empowering teams means delegating decision-making authority to those closest to the work. Providing teams with the necessary context and trusting them to make informed decisions can enhance efficiency and motivation.

Consider a scenario where a software development team regularly encounters delays due to a cumbersome and outdated deployment process. Instead of management dictating a specific solution, empowering the team would involve giving them the authority to research, propose, and implement a new deployment strategy. This could include choosing new deployment tools, redesigning the deployment pipeline, or adopting new practices like continuous deployment.

This approach recognizes that the team that knows the deployment process is best positioned to improve it based on their experience. It also makes the team more invested in the outcome than if there's just a top-down mandate. Allowing the team to experiment and take risks can lead to more innovative solutions than if decisions are made solely by management. It also speeds up decision-making, as there's no need for multiple rounds of external approval and feedback.

Note that this doesn't mean all decisions should or will fall to individual teams; some decisions properly belong at the organization or even business level. An empowered team will feel confident in providing input and feedback on those decisions when they have it.

② RAPID FEEDBACK

Rapid feedback can include frequent automated testing, continuous integration, code review, stakeholder reviews, and many other moments in the software development lifecycle where you need to decide whether to proceed or change course.

Delayed feedback results in rework, wasted time and effort, and missed opportunities. We get feedback from our tools, our peers, our stakeholders, and our customers; according to this principle, we want to solicit this feedback regularly and frequently rather than bundling up large chunks of work for one cumbersome and time-consuming mega-review.

When there is a need for an approval or review process, one of the best ways to ensure rapid feedback is to establish a feedback cadence so that there is never a large backlog of work to be reviewed. By reviewing smaller batches, future batches can be informed by the feedback on earlier batches, rather than working on a large batch of work and then learning at feedback time that you've missed the mark.

❸ OUTCOMES OVER OUTPUTS

Goals and success measurements should be based on outcomes, such as customer satisfaction or market share, rather than outputs, such as the number of features released, bugs closed, or story points completed. Incentivizing teams based on output volume can steer them to invest in quantity over business impact.

When you align team objectives with business outcomes and use metrics that reflect these outcomes, you encourage innovation and creative problem-solving, ensuring that the work contributes effectively to the organization's goals.

The table on the next page highlights key differences between the two approaches.

What we left out

There are a few topics you might expect to see in a book like this that aren't present — leadership, performance management, and compensation, to name a few. This was a deliberate

Aspect	Output-based approach	Outcome-based approach
Definition of success	The quantity of what is produced, such as features, documentation, or lines of code.	The impact on customer behavior and business results, such as improved customer satisfaction or increased sales.
Key metrics	Measures include the number of features deployed, code commit frequency, and deadlines met.	Measures include customer engagement metrics, conversion rates, market share, and revenue growth.
Development focus	Focus is on executing a predefined set of tasks and deliverables.	Focus is on validating hypotheses about customer needs and business value by delivering the smallest viable increment.
Feedback loop	Feedback is often related to whether the product is delivered on time and within budget.	Feedback is based on how well the product changes user behavior or improves key business metrics.
Decision-making	The progress of deliverables drives decisions according to the project timeline.	Decisions are driven by data and insights about what will move the needle on desired outcomes.
Approach to change	Changes are often viewed as a setback or a sign of planning failure.	Changes are viewed as opportunities to learn and pivot toward more impactful results.
Team alignment	Teams may work in silos, with each department focusing on their own set of deliverables.	Cross-functional teams work collaboratively, with a shared understanding that the goal is to achieve the desired outcomes.
Response to failure	When a feature or project does not meet the specifications or deadlines, it is considered a failure.	Failure is viewed as a learning opportunity that informs the next iteration and brings the team closer to achieving the outcomes.

choice to keep the book focused on the interaction among business outcomes, developer productivity, and developer experience.

Of course, leadership, performance management, and compensation do play a role in the satisfaction of your engineers, just like the technical tools they use. Although we don't address these topics at length, keep in mind that they can all be levers for improvement.

What to expect from this book

So far, we've surveyed the engineering effectiveness landscape and all the factors likely to make your situation inconveniently unique. We also looked at three ways of working — empowered teams, rapid feedback, and outcomes over outputs — that are key to any effectiveness effort.

In the next three chapters, we'll look at each of the areas of effectiveness we outlined above: business outcomes, developer productivity, and developer experience. In these chapters, we'll share guidance that's broadly applicable despite company differences. We'll conclude with a chapter that offers a loose roadmap encompassing all three areas to address organization-wide improvements in effectiveness.

Let's get to work. ✻

> You'll find resources related to the book at swarmia.com/build

Build: Elements of an Effective Software Organization

2. Business Outcomes

Effective software organizations focus their investments on the right outcomes.

Achieving business outcomes isn't solely about writing code or shipping new features; it requires delivering tangible results that align with business objectives, all while maintaining product quality, efficient feature delivery, operational stability, and user satisfaction.

In this chapter, we'll explore how to structure a software development organization. Then, we'll share a framework to guide engineering teams in balancing short-term gains with long-term sustainability. We'll wrap up by discussing practices for successful prioritization.

Organizing for outcomes

The structure of an organization plays an integral role in how well the organization can deliver business outcomes. An organization's job is to promote efficiency and productivity, communicate effectively with organization members and stakeholders, provide clarity in goals and alignment with business goals, and ultimately, deliver on those goals.

Teams exist to manage complexity

Teams, not individuals, are the atomic units that make up an engineering organization. In the beginning, an organization may have only one software development team, and there's little complexity to manage. Team members have touched most of the codebase, and the codebase is small and tidy enough. Everyone knows everyone.

However, as a company accumulates new customers, features, and business needs, the full scope of the software grows difficult for any single person to grasp. More and more of the company's software engineers have never touched critical parts of the software. Finding the right person to ask a technical question sometimes becomes a multi-day adventure.

This is why we have teams. By dividing into teams, an organization can take on more complex problems and tasks while effectively delivering business outcomes. The concept of a team allows a small group of people to feel connected with their objectives, codebase, and teammates.

> **By dividing into teams, an organization can take on more complex problems and tasks while effectively delivering business outcomes.**

At the same time, creating a team, by definition, creates a silo. When you put a group of people together, you're implicitly saying that it's more important for this group to be in sync with each other than with those outside the team. Silos are often considered in a negative light, but without some degree of siloing, everyone would have to pay attention to everything all the time, and things would undoubtedly fall between the cracks. With teams, we create focus and efficiency, even at the expense of more cross-team collaboration in some situations.

What is a team?

A team is more than a group of people assigned to work with each other. A viable team has common objectives and a clear understanding that success at those objectives requires team members to depend on and trust each other. Everyone on the team has clear roles and responsibilities without establishing rigid lines between how different team members contribute. Team members decide on the team's goals in a process that values and considers the input of one another, stakeholders, and dependent teams; the success of a team is measured against its goals and objectives.

Teams have team members, typically from disciplines including software engineering, product design, and product management, among others. This cross-functional approach helps foster a sense of ownership and collaboration across the team rather than different roles that work by handing work off from one person to another.

Perhaps most importantly, a team should be substantively able to deliver value to the organization using only the resources of that team. If a group of people can only create value in partnership with another group, they're not a team. Empowered teams are more resilient to organizational change and allow room for growth and development.

Tradeoffs in team design

There are four key areas to consider when you're designing teams within a software organization.

1. **Outcomes.** You need to align teams with the company's investment priorities and important business metrics, ensuring that the desired outcomes are being achieved efficiently.

2. **Features.** Every product area needs clear ownership in the form of a team responsible for its development, bug fixes, and improvements.

3. **People.** Healthy, effective teams include diverse viewpoints and skill sets, including those relating to software engineering, product management, and design.

4. **Architecture.** Conway's law reminds us that the user-facing systems we create tend to mirror the organizational structure that created them.

When these areas are well-defined, they establish the boundaries of a team's ownership and responsibilities. Creating effective teams involves evaluating tradeoffs in skill set requirements, dependencies on other teams, optimal team size, support and coaching needs, standardization, architectural support, and domain complexity. You'll almost never get it right the first time, so experimentation will be necessary before you land on a good mix.

> **Sometimes it's not feasible to include every skill set within a single team, leading to alternative solutions like formal or informal organizations for certain skills.**

Compromises will be necessary. Having one larger, more diverse team might be more practical than having two smaller but deeply interdependent teams (for example, a frontend team and a backend team). Sometimes it's not feasible to include every skill set within a single team, leading to alternative solutions like formal or informal organizations for certain skills. Sometimes the deployment target — for example, iOS — warrants a team all its own.

Effective teams tend to include engineers with experience across the stack. People whose experience with various aspects of software development — from data to systems design to frontend, if needed — can accelerate an engineering effort on multiple levels.

In cases where the codebase is complex and wasn't designed to be worked on by independent teams, you might need to address technical debt or even rearchitect parts of the system before you can achieve better scalability and team autonomy.

Different kinds of teams for different purposes

Developing an engineering organization requires understanding the distinct needs that different types of teams fill and the order in which to introduce each type of team. Here's a focused approach on how to strategically develop these teams, considering their unique purposes and contributions.

1 START WITH PRODUCT TEAMS

The initial manifestation of an engineering organization is typically a single product team. Product teams are fundamental in owning and managing specific slices of your business domain, allowing them to operate with a high degree of autonomy and minimal dependencies.

Product teams make decisions and deliver features that directly drive business outcomes. This model aligns with rapid and effective product development, as each team becomes responsible for a distinct product segment, ensuring focused and specialized attention to their respective areas.

Business Outcomes

In practice, product teams start by focusing on key business areas or customer segments. As the organization grows, these teams expand, diversifying into more specialized units while maintaining their core focus on their segment of the product.

As an organization evolves, product teams will be the most common type of team.

❷ INTEGRATE PLATFORM TEAMS

Once you have a few product teams, you'll often discover that they act like independent companies. On the one hand, this is by design; on the other hand, you generally don't want six product teams solving essentially the same hard problem in six different ways.

> **The idea with platform teams is that whatever your company is doing a lot of, it should get really good at doing.**

Some platform needs are common across almost all software companies. For example:

- CI/CD pipelines to get changes quickly and reliably to production.

- Design systems that make it easier for all frontend developers to build consistent interfaces.

- Scaffolding to deploy new microservices quickly in the company's cloud environment, with security and compliance requirements met and with a good developer experience.

However, some platform needs will be very specific to your company. The idea with platform teams is that *whatever your company is doing a lot of, it should get really good at doing*. These could be things like

- Tooling and libraries to visualize data in a data-heavy product.

- Ways to build integrations for an integration-heavy product, with tools like debugging webhooks and building authentication flows.

- Ways to tackle app performance issues so that teams can build features with less focus on scalability.

- Abstracting away unnecessary details of your business so that everyone can move faster.

No matter how important an objective is for your company, you can't suddenly assign a thousand engineers to work on it using systems built for 10 engineers and still expect results. To that end, large tech companies often invest 30-50% of their engineers in platform teams with the objective of allowing the rest of the engineers to move faster.

The evolution and eventual roster of platform teams can vary quite a bit from one organization to another. A single platform team can own many things. Still, eventually, you tend to see a platform team break into several sub-teams, each focused on providing a specific type of value to product team engineers.

③ INTRODUCE SPECIAL TEAMS

As the organization continues to scale, certain areas will emerge that don't fit neatly into existing product or platform team structures. This is where you may have to get creative and design another type of team.

Product teams and platform teams have fairly simple patterns of ownership and communication needs. At some point, you'll want to make a tradeoff that doesn't perfectly fit these models, and that's fine — as long as you recognize the tradeoff you're making.

A team might specialize in one of these aspects:

- **Enabling.** They could be helping the rest of your organization with security, recruiting, onboarding, or any other crucial aspect.

- **Complex subsystem.** Sometimes a system is important enough to warrant continuous investment in a team that maintains it

- **Temporary or project-based.** These teams are often formed to address specific challenges or objectives, and may be disbanded or reformed as goals are achieved or priorities change. This could be a big migration from yesterday's testing framework to whatever we do today. Be aware that they might leave behind code whose ownership is questionable.

- **Objective-driven.** Some teams are defined by specific objectives they aim to achieve, not by a product or codebase boundary. This could be a team that's focused on cross-cutting customer onboarding experience. A significant portion of the team's work involves collaborating in areas owned by other teams. This requires them to have strong cross-functional communication and coordination skills.

EVOLUTION OF TEAM STRUCTURES

The evolution of team structures in an engineering organization typically follows a progression from product teams to platform teams and eventually to special teams, as needed. This progression aligns with the growing complexity and diversifying needs of the business.

1. **Product teams.** The most common kind of team in an organization. Your organization's first team is almost certainly a product team. Product teams focus on specific business outcomes and product segments.

2. **Platform teams.** These are introduced to provide overarching support and standardization, enhancing the efficiency and cohesiveness of product teams. Typically, an organization has one platform team that may grow into its own platform organization.

3. **Special teams.** These emerge to address specific, cross-cutting objectives, filling any gaps in the organization and contributing to areas that require a broader, more integrated approach. An organization could have as few as zero special teams at any given time, depending on their business needs.

Each type of team addresses a distinct need within the organization, and their sequential introduction aligns with the natural growth and diversification of the organization's responsibilities and objectives.

Tradeoffs in organization design

When you're deciding how to structure and staff an organization, tradeoffs are inevitable. We talked above about how this works at the individual team level, but similar challenges exist when designing the organization as a whole.

Where you land on these decisions will depend on the stage of the company and the input of your stakeholders, among other factors. As you design and evolve your organization, you'll do well to ensure that you make intentional decisions about where you want to land in each of these areas.

- **Autonomy vs. coordination.** Autonomy can foster a culture of innovation and quick adaptation, allowing teams to respond rapidly to challenges and opportunities. Excessive autonomy can lead to inconsistent organizational practices and difficulties integrating work from different teams. Emphasizing cross-team coordination ensures that all parts of the organization are aligned and moving in the same direction. Still, it has the potential to slow down some decision-making processes and stifle innovation and ownership at the team level.

- **Specialists vs. generalists.** Specialists are essential for tackling complex, niche problems. A team composed solely of specialists might struggle with flexibility and cross-functional tasks. In contrast, generalists can work across various domains, providing the team with greater versatility, but they may lack the in-depth knowledge needed for certain tasks.

- **Centralized vs. distributed decision-making.** Centralized decision-making ensures a unified strategic direction and consistency in processes. However, it can lead to decision-making bottlenecks and a disconnection from the on-the-ground realities faced by teams. Distributed decision-making empowers teams, allowing for faster responses and a greater sense of ownership over outcomes. Yet, without sufficient coordination, this can lead to a lack of strategic alignment and varying approaches to similar problems across the organization.

- **Short-term delivery vs. long-term sustainability.** Prioritizing short-term delivery can achieve quick market gains and customer satisfaction, but it may come at the cost of accumulating technical debt. Conversely, focusing on the long-term sustainability of the architecture ensures a robust and scalable platform but could delay immediate product deliverables.

- **New features vs. maintenance.** New features keep the product competitive, but focusing solely on new development can neglect the necessary improvement and maintenance of existing features, potentially impacting reliability and customer satisfaction.

- **Large vs. small teams.** Larger teams can manage a wider range of tasks and bigger projects but may face challenges with agility and internal communication. Small teams, known for their agility and effective communication, can quickly adapt and innovate but may be limited in the scale of projects they can effectively manage.

- **New tech vs. existing solutions.** New technologies can offer strategic advantages and long-term benefits, positioning the company at the forefront of innovation. However, they come with risks and uncertainties. On the other hand, existing, proven technologies provide stability and predictability but may lack the advantages of newer solutions. (When in doubt, choose boring technology.)

The decisions you make here don't have to be permanent ones; you're going to get some things wrong, and decisions that were correct before will turn wrong over time. Don't stick a firm stake in the ground when deciding on these tradeoffs. Instead, identify where on the spectrum you want to be for each category and determine how well you're adhering to that — and how well it's serving you — over time.

Antipatterns for organization design

As you think about the different tradeoffs, there are plenty of antipatterns to avoid. Each of these antipatterns is a choice that very smart people have made in the past, but we recognize now that each of these choices sets you up for different kinds of struggles and failures.

- **Frontend and backend teams.** Most customer-facing features require both frontend and backend work. Dividing teams along these lines leads to a lack of collaboration, understanding, and ownership among different parts of the product development process. This separation often results in challenges with integrating the frontend and backend aspects of a project, typically leading to competing prioritization decisions by the different teams.

- **Multiple teams sharing a backlog.** Many engineers working from a single shared backlog can lead to prioritization issues, reduced ownership, and decreased clarity on individual contributions. When too many people are involved, it becomes challenging to manage dependencies and coordinate effectively, leading to bottlenecks and slowdowns. Additionally, this setup can dilute responsibility and accountability, as team members may not feel directly connected to the outcomes of their work.

- **Too many small teams.** While small teams are often more agile and efficient, over-fragmenting the engineering organization into too many tiny teams can lead to problems with coordination, culture, alignment, and consistency. A new team may need to be tiny at first, but teams of five to seven software engineers will be healthier and more sustainable over the long term.

- **Delivery teams.** These are teams that are solely responsible for delivering work specified by people outside the team. Without integrating cross-functional perspectives, they will tend to ship products that are technically sound but fail to meet user needs or business objectives.

- **Lack of clear areas of ownership.** When there is ambiguity about who owns specific parts of the product or codebase, it can lead to neglect of certain areas, especially maintenance and quality assurance, creating confusion during decision-making processes.

Roles and reporting lines

Typically, software engineers report to a line engineering manager. These leaders are familiar with the engineers' day-to-day work, providing guidance, oversight, and support. In a small or shallow organization, there could be very few additional layers between that line manager and the CEO or CTO. In a more mature or structured environment, more roles start to emerge. Not every organization will need every role, but these broad distinctions become fairly typical over time, and each has a part to play in an organization's effectiveness effort.

- **Senior software engineers.** They're usually expected to take projects from start to finish, alleviating the team leads or managers from micromanaging individual projects. This approach allows leaders to focus more on team dynamics and strategic planning. Importantly, they rarely work alone; their leadership comes from being a force multiplier for the team by guiding and mentoring others. They advise junior team members, enhance team skills and cohesion, and play a critical role in maintaining high quality standards.

- **Staff+.** Staff+ engineers function as leaders within the larger engineering organization but without direct people management responsibilities. Their scope typically extends beyond a single team, setting operational standards and guiding architecture across a portion of the group or organization. Staff+ engineers set operational standards and guide architectural decisions that ensure scalability and efficiency. They influence technical strategy, align it with business goals, and mentor other engineers, elevating the overall technical skills of the organization. Often, they report to a manager at a higher level than the manager of the team they work most closely with.

- **Line engineering managers.** Successful people in this role have a strong understanding of software development, usually through several years of hands-on experience. They ensure that the team has what it needs to be successful and coordinate with other teams in the organization. Through one-on-ones and other techniques, they use coaching and performance conversations to support career progression while often still providing technical guidance. They may partner with a Staff+ engineer for technical guidance as well. This role is pivotal in organizations where individual teams require focused managerial and technical support, ensuring that the technical execution and team well-being are prioritized

- **Senior managers and directors.** Typically, they're responsible for several teams, with line engineering managers reporting to them. As part of managing their organization, they're likely responsible for headcount, budget planning, performance management, organization design, cross-team alignment, higher-level goal setting, inter- and intra-organization optimizations, and so much more — the role can vary greatly by company stage and size, and even within internal organizations. People in this role typically aren't hands-on in day-to-day software engineering work; indeed, a major challenge is to stay connected to the realities of that work while doing the rest of the job. They tend to report to senior directors, a vice president, a head of engineering, or sometimes the CEO or CTO.

- **VPs and CTOs.** VPs tend to be execution-oriented, while CTOs focus on providing a strategic and technical vision. Depending on the organization, the overall engineering vision and strategy usually come from someone in one of these roles, and the vision they provide aligns with the company's long-term goals. Either of these roles can lead an engineering organization, make high-level decisions on technology and product development, and ensure that the engineering team scales in line with the company's growth. Each role is crucial in fostering innovation, driving technical excellence, and ensuring that engineering practices contribute effectively to the company's objectives.

Product roles also have a tremendous influence on an effectiveness effort. These roles often report separately from engineering roles, but individual product managers and product designers are assigned to individual teams.

Teams as a strategic investment

High-performing teams are an exception, not the rule. They don't just happen — they require time to form, good leadership to maintain motivation, and clear areas of ownership and autonomy.

Not long ago — and certainly some companies still do this! — teams were organized around a set of features that needed to be built. Team members had input on the technical implementation but little involvement in defining how the feature would work, and often sought (and received) little feedback on whether their work had the desired outcome. The work was the outcome.

In contemporary thinking, teams are conceived not just as functional units executing predetermined tasks but instead as strategic investments. This shift recognizes teams not as stops on an assembly line but rather as fundamental drivers of business success, where their focus is on understanding users, not just on the features or products they develop.

> **High-performing teams require time to form, good leadership to remain motivated, and clear areas of ownership and autonomy.**

Once again, empowered teams — a table stake we mentioned in Chapter 1 — are essential to making this work, and those teams need to be held accountable for the outcomes they achieve. Teams that can adapt and respond to new information and changing conditions will perform best in this scenario.

Investing in teams means more than just providing tasks; it involves nurturing their growth, capabilities, and cohesion. This includes:

- **Skill development.** Continuous learning and development opportunities help teams stay ahead of the curve, both technically and in terms of industry knowledge.

- **Cultivating culture.** A strong team culture that fosters collaboration, innovation, and a sense of ownership is crucial. The team's values and norms should align with those of the larger organization.

- **Resource allocation.** Ensuring teams have the necessary resources — from tools and technology to sufficient staffing — is a key aspect of treating the team as an investment.

> **Investing in teams means more than just providing tasks; it involves nurturing their growth, capabilities, and cohesion.**

Again, the team, not the individual, is the fundamental unit of an engineering organization and a powerful lever for improving an organization's effectiveness. Designing an outcome-oriented organization demands that you consider team and organization shape, as both influence how effectively work gets done.

Balancing engineering investments

In 2020, **Matt Eccleston**, a former Dropbox VP of Engineering, spelled out a framework for balancing and budgeting engineering resourcing. Our adaptation of this is what we call the Balance Framework. The Balance Framework is a model for understanding the distribution of an engineering organization's efforts. It categorizes the organization's work into four main areas: ❶ **new things** (creating new features or services), ❷ **improving things** (enhancing current features, services, and business processes), ❸ **keeping the lights on (KTLO)** (maintaining existing systems and services), and ❹ **productivity work** (making it easier to get work done).

One of the most potent aspects of the Balance Framework is its ability to create a shared language for people to use across various organizational roles, such as engineering, product, and senior leadership. This shared language allows for improved communication, aligning objectives, prioritizing work, and tracking progress more efficiently.

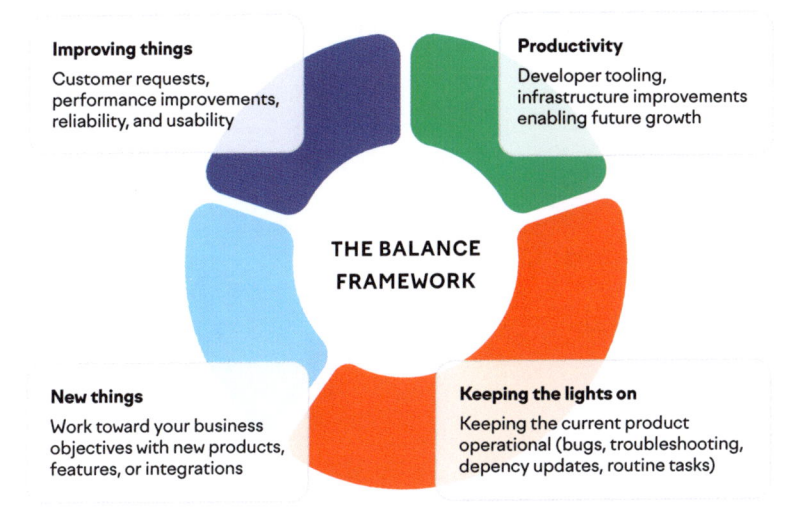

Improving things
Customer requests, performance improvements, reliability, and usability

Productivity
Developer tooling, infrastructure improvements enabling future growth

THE BALANCE FRAMEWORK

New things
Work toward your business objectives with new products, features, or integrations

Keeping the lights on
Keeping the current product operational (bugs, troubleshooting, depency updates, routine tasks)

LET'S LOOK AT EACH CATEGORY MORE CLOSELY:

1. **New things.** Developing new features, products, or services. This represents innovation, exploring new market opportunities, and expanding product offerings.

2. **Improving things.** Enhancing current features, services, tools, and business processes. This could be optimizing a feature for better user experience or revamping a service for improved performance.

3. **Keeping the lights on.** Keeping existing systems running effectively and efficiently. This includes bug fixes, system maintenance, and dealing with technical debt.

4. **Productivity work.** Improving skills, optimizing workflows, upgrading tools, and creating an environment that allows the team to work at its best.

Investing too heavily in any one category can lead to problems. For example, focusing too much on new things at the expense of KTLO could result in system instability and a decreased ability to deliver work due to technical debt. Conversely, excessive focus on KTLO might result in fewer new things and improvements, leading to a stagnating product

> **A healthy blend tends to include at least 10% for productivity work and between 10% and 30% for KTLO work.**

and missed opportunities for innovation and improvement. A healthy blend tends to include at least 10% for productivity work and between 10% and 30% for KTLO work. The remaining time investment will depend on the nature of your business and your product strategy.

Balancing at the team level

Never forget that a quarter, a half, and a year all have a finite number of days in them. In a quarter, there are 13 weeks, or 65 working days. When thinking about what a team can get done, remember that some percentage of that time needs to be held back for slack time (to address KTLO and reactive work), vacation time, and holidays. A team of five that starts with a theoretical 325 available engineering days in a quarter may end up having as less than half of that time available to invest in the new things and improving things category.

With that in mind, teams should also be thoughtful and intentional about how they invest their time in different areas, even if the exact breakdown doesn't match the organization-level investment levels. Setting an investment balance intention at the team level can help make future decisions more straightforward.

Fostering collaboration with the Balance Framework

The Balance Framework emphasizes that improving productivity is a collaborative effort among engineering, product management, and product design. It creates a shared language between the diverse roles involved in product development, from software engineers to the CFO.

It also empowers engineers to advocate for the kind of productivity work that often goes overlooked and understand the value of the new things they're building. A specific allocation for improvements allows product managers and designers to make strategic near-term investments that will pay off in the long run instead of always prioritizing shiny new features. All this ensures that customer-reported issues are addressed while fostering a sense of ownership over the product among engineers, promoting a more engaged team.

Other stakeholders benefit too. Finance can use the information for forecasting and reporting. Given competing priorities, sales and marketing can use this information to understand how much feature development they can expect.

In a smaller organization, conversations around impact and priorities can happen organically; in a larger one, whole departments might exist for each role, making communication more challenging. Having a standard language through the Balance Framework saves you the pain of unintended miscommunication and helps you align priorities between stakeholders.

Using the Balance Framework to improve effectiveness

You can use the Balance Framework to set organizational, team, or even individual intentions around how time gets spent, as well as to give business leaders the visibility they need to determine where engineering effort is going.

With the Balance Framework, you might set a goal for an organization to reduce its KTLO investment from 40% to 20% by the end of the year while maintaining or improving quality metrics. Specific teams can put an additional 20% of their efforts into productivity by addressing technical debt and implementing automation. Product (improving things and new things) will only get 40% investment until the KTLO burden diminishes; the product team buys faster feature delivery in the future by accepting slower feature delivery today.

This example highlights essential tensions in software engineering, mainly because you always have only 100% to spend. If the team previously spent 0% of their time on the productivity improvements category, then that 20% has to come from the other three categories. In this example, product work initially got 60% of the organization's attention; dropping that to 40% will hurt a bit.

The main challenge of the Balance Framework is that it requires you to adopt a taxonomy when labeling work across your engineering processes so that you can associate each unit of work with a Balance Framework category. The easier you make it for engineers to label their work, the more likely you will get trustworthy data. You may want to adjust the exact classifications — for example, it may be helpful to differentiate productivity improvement work from feature improvement work — but try to keep it to just a handful of adjustments.

Once the data starts to flow, you can also begin to use it to set team and individual intentions. For example, you can identify whether one person on your team is doing all the KTLO. If so, it may become a team or individual priority to spread that burden more evenly.

What to do when you're drowning in KTLO

If you're dealing with a substantial amount of KTLO work, it's a clear sign that something needs to change. KTLO tasks are those necessary to maintain the existing systems and processes, and while they are essential, excessive KTLO can limit a team's ability to innovate and deliver new value.

You can employ a few approaches if a team is swamped with KTLO work.

- **Prioritize and delegate.** Not all KTLO work is equally important. The team should take time to evaluate their KTLO tasks and prioritize them based on their business impact. The low-priority, non-strategic tasks could be automated, outsourced, or temporarily ignored, allowing the team to focus on higher-impact tasks.

- **Invest in automation.** If a significant proportion of KTLO tasks are routine and repetitive, the team could invest in automation. This may involve using existing tools or developing custom solutions. Automating repetitive tasks can free up significant time, allowing the team to focus on more strategic work.

- **Reduce technical debt.** Too much KTLO work could be the result of substantial technical debt. For example, a codebase that's full of one-off exceptions for individual customers can make any change risky; this variance should be managed via configuration, not code. Regularly allocating time to reduce technical debt — through refactoring, improving test coverage, updating documentation, etc. — can reduce the amount of KTLO work over time.

- **Reconsider the product roadmap.** If KTLO tasks are hindering progress, it might be time to revisit the product roadmap. Balancing new features and improvements against maintenance tasks is crucial to ensure the team can deliver on strategic objectives over the long term.

- **Ask for more resources.** If KTLO tasks are overwhelming and the strategies above aren't enough, the team might need more help. This could mean hiring more team members, reallocating resources from other parts of the organization, or using third-party service providers.

When you're inundated with KTLO, it can be tempting to take shortcuts or make hasty decisions to lighten the load. Victory will be fleeting if you choose tactics like working longer hours or taking solely a firefighting approach. Quick "fixes" often exacerbate the very issues they aim to solve, adding to technical debt and leading to burnout among software engineers.

Similarly, prioritizing new features at the expense of KTLO tasks, or hastily outsourcing these tasks without proper oversight, can create more problems down the line. The key to effectively managing KTLO work isn't simply to eliminate KTLO tasks but to approach them strategically, keeping in mind their impact on long-term product goals and the well-being of the team.

Setting priorities

Every engineering organization, no matter its size, struggles with managing competing requests from stakeholders. It's common to see an organization trying to decide among very different types of work. For example, finance wants engineering to cut cloud spend, product wants engineering to build things that drive customer value, and engineering wants engineering to pay down its technical debt.

> **With a poor prioritization strategy — or none at all — you end up with multiple competing high-priority goals.**

With a poor prioritization strategy — or none at all — you end up with multiple competing high-priority goals. In the above scenario, if you choose to say yes to all three things, it's entirely possible that none of them actually gets done because engineering's finite time is split across three major projects when there is only room for one. Not only is this bad for the business, but it's also painful for the engineers who are trying to do all the work. Quickly, you'll see signs of:

- **Priority fatigue/burnout.** Engineers will no longer rally around top priorities even when needed since everything is a top priority. Instead, they just "do some work and go home."

- **Hiding work.** Engineers will start hiding work from product management or including unnecessary work in product increments, e.g. "We can't do this one-week thing unless we spend two weeks refactoring the whole thing."

- **Withholding feedback on priorities.** When engineers feel like prioritization is poor and nothing is changing, they often stop giving feedback. Leadership will only see the effects of poor prioritization on teams and struggle to understand the underlying issues that led to those effects.

Any one of these things can be poison to an effectiveness effort — they will make meeting the table stakes mentioned in Chapter 1 almost impossible.

Setting priorities is more than just ranking a list of tasks in order of importance. True priorities should highlight the areas where effort will have the most impact on the organization's goals.

When something is a priority, that doesn't necessarily mean that every engineer is continually engaged in working toward that priority. Rather, saying something is a priority implies a strategic alignment of choices, where team members, when presented with options, prioritize work that contributes to these key areas. When priorities are clear, the organization focuses on strategic outcomes while day-to-day operations continue without major disruption.

At every level of the business, priorities must be informed by product and business strategy. While empowered teams should be setting their own local priorities, these priorities must be informed by the product and business strategy — and vice versa. Effective prioritization requires knowledge and insights to flow in both directions, so team input should also inform priorities at the group, organization, and even business levels.

OKRs: A framework to communicate priorities

Priorities don't matter much if they're not communicated clearly. The Objectives and Key Results (OKR) framework, described by former Intel leader **John Doerr** in his book *Measure What Matters*, has emerged as a common tool for communicating priorities across an organization and tracking progress on those priorities. However, the effectiveness of this approach varies across different levels of the business and depends a lot on making sure that the overhead doesn't outweigh the benefits.

We like to think of OKRs as a "high-five" standard; if we accomplish this, will the organization, group, or team have a moment when they all high-five each other (at least metaphorically)? OKRs should be achievable but ambitious. They should be based on outcomes, not a list of tasks to be completed or outputs to be created.

For example, consider a business objective to "hold the line on churn," with key results of 95% net revenue retention across the customer base and 99% retention among the top 100 customers. Just like any good objective, it doesn't tell you how to achieve these things — that falls to the teams and groups across the entire organization. It also doesn't tell you who will do the work; efforts toward business-level objectives will often involve marketing, sales, product, and engineering (at least).

With this in mind, OKRs immediately present the challenge of managing cross-team and cross-organization work. We'll discuss this challenge in more detail below, but at a high level, what we've seen work well is a system where the engineering organization also has OKRs, and those OKRs closely reflect company OKRs. Within an engineering organization, each objective and key result may be owned by a group or team.

So, in the above example, an engineering organization might set OKRs such as the following.

- **Objective: Hold the line on churn**
    - Reach five 9s of API uptime in a running 30-day window to address frequent user complaints.
    - Measure and improve ongoing engagement with users via messaging apps and emails.
    - Support a +20% YoY improvement in net revenue retention among the top 100 customers.

For some teams in the organization, these OKRs could directly intersect with their area of ownership, and they should prioritize their work accordingly. Still, OKRs should never create an all-hands-on-deck situation; part of using OKRs responsibly is accepting and explicitly acknowledging that they will never cover the full scope of work that should be happening.

A clever senior leader may share a list of OKRs but then declare, "Security is always our top priority" (or cost cutting, or KTLO, or something else that didn't end up on the OKR list). Sometimes product and engineering will each come up with separate OKRs. If you have two lists of five top objectives, you have 10 top objectives. There must be one short list at the highest level, and everything on it should be material to the success of the business. Otherwise, every level below has to choose who to please and who to offend.

> **Part of using OKRs responsibly is accepting and explicitly acknowledging that they will never cover the full scope of work that should be happening.**

An efficient OKR process is marked by minimal overhead, with individual teams spending less than a week per quarter on OKR-related tasks. While the OKR approach does require aligning with other teams, the alignment process should not be about crafting a perfectly cascading plan across the organization but rather about ensuring that there is harmony in direction and purpose.

As you evaluate OKR progress, watch out for "watermelon status," where the outward reporting of progress does not match the actual data, indicating a disconnect between perception and reality. Keep watch also for objectives that focus on an output or checklist vs. a specific business outcome.

OKRs must be part of a larger discussion involving investment balance and organizational design. Imposing an OKR process on a team that is under-resourced or misaligned with the company's broader goals can lead to frustration and inefficiency. Your goal should be integrating OKRs into the organizational fabric, ensuring they complement and enhance the overall strategic direction and resource allocation *without* becoming a source of debilitating overhead.

At the business and organization level, OKRs excel in setting clear directions and establishing priorities. They are designed to focus on a few crucial objectives, ensuring a focused effort where it matters most. As discussed above, the key results associated with these objectives steer clear of dictating the how, focusing instead on what the achievements will look like upon completion.

Applying OKRs at the group level brings challenges, particularly in organizations where trust is low. There's often a tendency to develop group-level OKRs that cover every team, lest some teams feel overlooked or undervalued. Furthermore, the very structure of some organizations can make it challenging to establish shared objectives that resonate across all teams.

TEAM-LEVEL OKRS

At the team level, OKRs are useful for communicating and aligning with leadership and other teams, leaving the details to the team to work out while creating visibility for leaders. Be careful, though: the practicality of OKRs at the team level can be outweighed if you're spending too much time developing them.

Measurement paralysis is a frequent challenge, as a team spends time figuring out how to measure the impact of an issue rather than simply resolving it. Another challenge of OKRs at the team level is that they need to serve audiences up, out, and down. Coming up with language that accurately represents work to the team, its stakeholders, and its management chain can be (and can create) far more trouble than it's worth.

Another shortcoming of OKRs is that the "ambitious but achievable" standard doesn't work as well for KTLO work. The

OKR framework described by Doerr excludes this kind of work, focusing only on new business objectives. When OKRs focus only on new work, a team or individual can end up in a situation where their extremely necessary KTLO work is undervalued.

> **Measurement paralysis is a frequent challenge, as a team spends time figuring out how to measure the impact of an issue rather than simply resolving it.**

OKRs also don't include reactive work — the stuff that comes up that's difficult to predict ahead of time. This could be anything from a security issue in a software library or a production incident to a last-minute request from a VP to gather some data.

Finally, don't ask teams to create new OKRs every quarter or on any particular cadence. At the team level, a light and occasional refresh should be sufficient. Otherwise, team OKRs often become more like to-do lists than strategic objectives, providing little value as a communication tool. The time invested in developing and tracking these OKRs can be extensive, and the benefits might not always be proportional.

A NOTE ON OKRS FOR PLATFORM TEAMS

Platform groups face a unique scenario when it comes to OKRs. These groups find OKRs most beneficial when the group thinks of itself as owning a product rather than just maintaining a set of services or capabilities.

For more service-oriented teams, OKRs can feel irrelevant because much of their work tends to be KTLO-shaped.

Depending on their nature, platform teams may be a case where standard OKR practices don't make much sense. Here and elsewhere, in the interest of empowered teams, listen closely to the team if it struggles to communicate its planned work this way.

Managing cross-team initiatives

One of the hardest prioritization challenges for a software company is cross-team projects. It's rarely convenient for people across teams to suddenly work on the same thing at the same time, especially if the value of that work to the team's users isn't very clear. It's imperative to keep people on the same page about the importance of the project and to understand project progress across teams.

> **It's imperative to keep people on the same page about the importance of the project and to understand project progress across teams.**

Successfully and predictably leading complex, cross-cutting initiatives in a software engineering organization requires timely, accurate, trustworthy data about the work that's being done toward completing the initiative. With that knowledge in hand, you can ensure that progress is made with a reasonable scope and a reasonable amount of engineering resources.

If things aren't moving along as quickly as you'd hope, there are a few common culprits you can look for and address.

- **Doing too many things at once.** When teams try to handle too many tasks simultaneously, it leads to interruptions and context switching, drastically reducing productivity and focus. Team members become overwhelmed, leading to a decrease in work quality and delays in project timelines. Teams need to prioritize tasks, define specific focus areas, and implement work-in-progress limits. Advocate for realistic planning based on the team's scope and obligations; leaders should limit the number of initiatives a team is expected to work on at any given time.

- **Working on increments that are too large.** Large increments can extend development cycles, reducing the team's ability to adapt to changes and delaying feedback. This approach can also overwhelm the team and make it challenging to track progress. Teams should break down work into small increments — tasks that can be completed in one or two days. Smaller increments allow for quicker feedback, easier adjustments, and clearer demonstration of progress. Small increments are also proven to increase overall throughput.

- **Relying on individuals vs. the team.** When an initiative depends excessively on a single person, bottlenecks and delays arise when those individuals are overloaded or unavailable. This pattern also undermines team collaboration and knowledge sharing. Leaders at every level must encourage a team-oriented approach where knowledge and responsibilities are shared. Incorporate cross-training and collaborative work practices to ensure the team can make progress even when key individuals are absent.

- **Failing to incorporate new information.** When a team sticks too rigidly to a plan without adapting to new information or changing circumstances, you end up with outdated solutions and missed opportunities. Promote and cultivate a growth mindset, encouraging teams to revisit and revise plans as new information becomes available.

- **Focusing on outputs over outcomes.** When initiatives are evaluated solely on outputs (like the number of story points or features completed), it's easy to lose sight of the actual goals of the initiative, such as improving user satisfaction or increasing sales. This misalignment can lead to inefficiencies and time spent on work that doesn't contribute to the objective. Focus instead on the outcomes the project is trying to achieve. Set clear (preferably user/customer-centric) goals, and measure progress toward them to ensure that work aligns with the project's desired outcome(s).

- **Ignoring hidden work and KTLO work.** Often, there's significant work involved in maintaining existing systems that goes unnoticed or underestimated. Ignoring this aspect can strain resources and impact the delivery of new projects. Account for maintenance and operational work when planning initiatives and adjust your expectations as needed as the initiative proceeds.

What's next?

In this chapter, we emphasized the strategic connection between software development and business objectives, and highlighted the Balance Framework as a key tool for managing resource allocation across near-term and long-term goals. We also explored the evolution and role of different team types — product, platform, and special teams — in effectively handling organizational complexity and driving business outcomes. We looked at examples of tradeoffs in team design and organizational structure, and tactics for prioritizing and managing cross-team efforts.

In the next two chapters, we'll talk about developer productivity and developer experience — two sides of the same coin that are both essential to a successful, sustainable software development organization. Business outcomes will suffer in the long run without investment in both areas. ✸

FURTHER READING

Accelerate: The Science of Lean Software and DevOps: Building and Scaling High Performing Technology Organizations, by **Dr. Nicole Forsgren**, **Jez Humble**, and **Gene Kim**. A foundational read for understanding the practices and capabilities that lead to high performance in software organizations.

Team Topologies: Organizing Business and Technology Teams for Fast Flow, by **Matthew Skelton** and **Manuel Pais**. A practical guide for designing team structures in software organizations, aligning with the principles of effective teamwork and outcome orientation.

Good Strategy Bad Strategy: The Difference and Why It Matters, by **Richard Rumelt**. An essential book for understanding the fundamentals of strategic planning and execution.

Mindset: The New Psychology of Success, by **Carol S. Dweck**. Explores the concept of mindset, distinguishing between a fixed mindset (believing that abilities are static) and a growth mindset (believing that abilities can be developed through hard work and dedication). Dweck argues that adopting a growth mindset leads to greater success and fulfillment

The Phoenix Project: A Novel about IT, DevOps, and Helping Your Business Win, by **Gene Kim**, **Kevin Behr**, and **George Spafford**. A highly readable novel that provides insights into DevOps practices and the importance of collaboration between development and business.

Measure What Matters: How Google, Bono, and the Gates Foundation Rock the World with OKRs, by **John Doerr**. Dig into the OKR framework with its creator.

The Manager's Path: A Guide for Tech Leaders Navigating Growth and Change, by **Camille Fournier**. A practical guide for engineering leaders, focusing on the challenges of managing technical teams and projects.

Writing an Engineering Strategy, by **Will Larson**. Larson writes extensively on engineering leadership, team organization, and technology management, providing valuable insights for software development leaders.
lethain.com/eng-strategies/

Choose Boring Technology, by **Dan McKinley**. This post advocates for the careful selection of technology in business and introduces the concept of innovation tokens, recommending that companies spend these sparingly and only on technologies that provide a significant advantage.
mcfunley.com/choose-boring-technology

A Framework for Balancing and Budgeting Engineering Resourcing, by **Matt Eccleston**. Discusses the importance of balancing different types of engineering investments to ensure long-term success and sustainability.
medium.com/engineering-operations/a-framework-for-balancing-and-budgeting-engineering-resourcing-d0cce0e6911c

Build: Elements of an Effective
Software Organization

3.

Developer
Productivity

✳

Effective software organizations
make fast and consistent progress
toward their goals.

The unfortunate reality about complexity in software is that if you just continue doing what you've always been doing, you'll keep slowing down. When starting a fresh project, you'll be surprised by how much you can accomplish in a day or two. In some other, more established environments, you could spend a week trying to get a new database column added.

Many things that slow down work are systemic, not individual. Even the most talented engineer might not fully understand how much time is wasted when work is bounced between teams, half-completed features are shelved as priorities change, or all the code gets reviewed by just one person. It's easy to think you're solving a quality problem by introducing code freezes and release approvals, but you might only be making things worse.

In this chapter, we'll talk about some of the perils of measuring productivity before we move on to the mechanics of making it happen in a way that's perceived as broadly beneficial.

But first, let's talk about the biggest question of all: what is productivity, anyway?

Defining developer productivity

If you ask a group of seasoned engineering leaders to define developer productivity, there will typically be no unified answer. For the purposes of this book, we consider developer productivity in the context of how organizations can minimize the time and effort required in the software delivery process to create valuable business outcomes. We will focus primarily on team- or service-level delivery and eliminating bottlenecks — often process bottlenecks — in the software delivery process.

> **A healthy productivity effort should not require a certain number of pull requests for each engineer every week.**

We'll also center our conversation on aggregate productivity instead of the efforts and contributions of individuals. A healthy productivity effort may involve automating more parts of the team's deployment process, addressing flaky tests that cause failing builds, or just getting a team to commit to reviewing open pull requests before starting on their own work. A healthy productivity effort should *not*, on the other hand, require a certain number of pull requests for each engineer every week. That approach is unlikely to create business value and very likely to create a toxic environment.

Productivity table stakes

Just as we discussed organizational table stakes in the first chapter — empowered teams, rapid feedback, and outcomes over output — there are three clear ways of working that you'll see on any highly productive team.

1. **Limited queue depth.** Controlling the number of tasks waiting to be processed (also known as a backlog) reduces lead times, improves predictability, and smooths the flow of work, thereby increasing efficiency and reducing the risk of bottlenecks.

2. **Small batch sizes.** Smaller batches of work are processed more quickly and with less variability, leading to faster feedback and reduced risk. This approach enhances learning and allows for more rapid adjustments to the product.

3. **Limited work-in-progress (WIP).** By restricting the number of tasks in progress at any given time, teams can focus better, reduce context switching, and accelerate the completion of tasks, thus improving overall throughput.

LIMITED QUEUE DEPTH

It's okay to admit it: we've all added a task to a backlog with a vague certainty that it will never get done.

Limiting queue depth means rigorously monitoring and managing the number of tasks awaiting work. This involves implementing systems to track and control the queue size, such as using a Kanban board to visualize work and enforce limits on the number of items in each stage. This principle also means you can't let backlogs grow unchecked, as this can lead to delays, rushed work, and increased stress.

Regularly review your work queues and adjust priorities to ensure that valuable and time-sensitive tasks are getting addressed promptly. When you encourage teams to complete current tasks before taking on new ones and use metrics like cycle time to identify bottlenecks, you can significantly enhance the flow and efficiency of the development process.

Implementing this in practice usually means limiting the number of tasks awaiting development, review, or deployment at any given time. In addition to providing clarity about what to work on next, this practice also dramatically improves the predictability of delivery once something reaches that initial awaiting development status.

SMALL BATCH SIZES

Breaking down large projects into smaller, more manageable parts allows for quicker completion of each part, enabling faster feedback and iterative improvements. For instance, deploying completed tasks incrementally rather than releasing a large set at once makes it easier to release more tasks in a given period of time; regressions will tend to be small, readily attributed, and readily fixed without blocking other tasks.

Large batches often complicate integration and make it difficult to track down problems. A continuous delivery model, where small updates are released whenever they're ready, is a practical application of this principle. Encourage teams to think in terms of small changes, which helps in managing risk and improving the ability to adapt to new information.

LIMITED WIP

When you introduce and regularly monitor WIP limits, you ensure that teams focus on completing ongoing tasks before starting new ones. Overloading team members with multiple tasks leads to reduced focus and increased cycle times. A culture where teams are encouraged to complete current work before embarking on new tasks improves focus, reduces waste, and speeds up work delivery.

The Kanban process embraces this explicitly, although you don't need to use Kanban to follow this principle. In that process, the team always focuses on completing the team's in-flight tasks before starting new ones — a process sometimes called "walking the board from right to left" — to encourage teammates to help each other before starting a new task. Similarly, scrum limits the number of story points in an individual sprint.

> A culture where teams are encouraged to complete current work before embarking on new tasks improves focus, reduces waste, and speeds up work delivery.

In the absence of WIP limits, a team can quickly start to juggle more than it can reasonably handle, and it's common for tasks to remain in progress for an extended period even though they aren't being actively worked upon.

Productivity vs. quality

A common misconception is that productivity and quality are in tension. If your version of quality is to manually test every change you make and test your whole product before releasing it, there will naturally be tension between the two. Any scenario that relies heavily on manual testing often leads to the creation of more processes — like a definition-of-done checklist on every pull request — further delaying time to value.

Fascinatingly, one of the best ways to achieve developer productivity involves improving the quality of your product through automated testing. If you're doing productivity right, quality will tend to increase over time, as it becomes easier to ship smaller changes and easier to roll back or disable features.

Broadly, this involves four things.

- **Make it easy to write tests.** Most programming languages have somewhat standard testing frameworks, and many software frameworks also come with clear patterns for testing. Educate your engineers on how to use these testing tools, making setup easy.

- **Make it easy to get the right data.** Tests shouldn't be talking to production to get data, but they need data that's a realistic simulation of the kind you'd see in production. If you ask individual engineers to solve the data problem independently, their approaches will be varied and surprising (and often quite bad).

- **Make it easy to manually test.** While you want to limit the amount of manual testing we're doing, there are lots of situations during the development of a feature where you'd like to be able to kick the tires and see how it works — for example, to show something to a product partner or another developer working remotely. Make it easy to interact with code that's on a feature branch.

- **Make it easy to release (and roll back) small changes.** One of the reasons teams get in a position of doing a ton of pre-release manual testing is that the release process itself is so onerous — and the rollback process is worse. Individual tasks stack up so that a release includes dozens of changes and tens of thousands of lines of code. When you make it trivial to release small changes, engineers will start making smaller changes, leading to vastly less risk for any given release.

If you've put these pieces in place — which can be harder than it sounds — you've given your engineers powerful tools that make their job easier, and you've also taken a big step toward a better product. Add a ratchet to CI to make sure test coverage of your code only goes up, and incentivize writing tests and sharing strategies within and across teams.

Once again, team structure (as discussed in Chapter 2) comes into play. Establishing a culture of (automated) quality requires that your teams have sufficient domain knowledge in testing methods for the language or framework being used. Emphasizing automated testing also encourages you to limit the complexity any single team has to deal with, so you in turn limit the surfaces they need to test.

Frameworks for thinking about productivity

There are a couple of frameworks that can be useful when considering the broad topic of productivity.

The DevOps Research and Assessment (DORA) framework has become a standard in the productivity realm for a reason: it offers a set of valuable metrics that shed light on where engineering teams might be able to improve their software delivery. By providing a baseline that captures a team's current state, DORA sets the benchmark for your team's processes. The aim isn't to become obsessed with numbers but to continually evaluate whether you're satisfied with what the numbers are telling you.

The success of the DORA framework — which originated from work by **Nicole Forsgren**, **Jez Humble**, and **Gene Kim** — lies in its simplicity and ability to capture various aspects of software development through its four core metrics:

1 lead time for changes, **2 deployment frequency**, **3 time to restore service**, and **4 change failure rate**. These metrics are in healthy tension with each other, which means improving one could unintentionally lead to the degradation of another.

Of course, there are limitations to the DORA metrics. While they offer a snapshot of your team's performance, they don't explain *why* something might be off. Nor do they tell you how to improve. The DORA framework is not a diagnostic tool; it doesn't point out bottlenecks in your processes or identify cultural issues inhibiting your team's effectiveness. It's much like having a compass — it will tell you what direction you're headed in, but not what obstacles lie in the way or how to navigate around them.

> **Unlike DORA, SPACE embraces quantitative and qualitative metrics, identifying five critical dimensions of software delivery and operational performance.**

The SPACE framework, developed by **Forsgren** along with **Margaret-Anne Storey**, **Chandra Maddila**, **Thomas Zimmerman**, **Brian Houck**, and **Jenna Butler**, grew out of an attempt to create a more comprehensive tool to capture the complex and interrelated aspects of software delivery and operations. The goal was to create a model that would acknowledge the competing tensions within software development and use those tensions as catalysts for improvement.

Unlike DORA, SPACE embraces quantitative and qualitative metrics, identifying five critical dimensions of software delivery and operational performance. The acronym stands for satisfaction, performance, activity, communication and collaboration, and efficiency and flow.

- **(S) Satisfaction** is how fulfilled and satisfied engineers feel about their work, team, tools, and culture. It also involves evaluating how that sentiment affects their engagement and fulfillment based on the work they do.

- **(P) Performance** evaluates whether the output of the engineering organization has the desired outcome relative to the investment. For example, what is the ROI of adding 20 engineers to an organization? This is notoriously difficult to measure in a concrete way when it comes to software engineering, meaning it's more of a theoretical concept than a roadmap to specific metrics.

- **(A) Activity** is a count of actions or outputs completed while performing work. These include outputs like design documents and actions like incident mitigation, as well as commits, pull requests, and code review comments.

- **(C) Communication & collaboration** captures how people and teams communicate and work together.

- **(E) Efficiency & flow** captures the ability to complete work or make progress on it with minimal interruptions or delays, whether individually or through a system.

SPACE offers a comprehensive (though fuzzy) approach to improving productivity. It acknowledges the interplay between different aspects of software development and provides a balanced and holistic model for assessment and improvement. Still, it is just a framework — it doesn't offer any specifics about what exactly to measure or what "good" should look like.

THE SPACE FRAMEWORK

- **S** — Satisfaction
- **P** — Performance
- **A** — Activity
- **C** — Communication & collaboration
- **E** — Efficiency & flow

PRODUCTIVITY

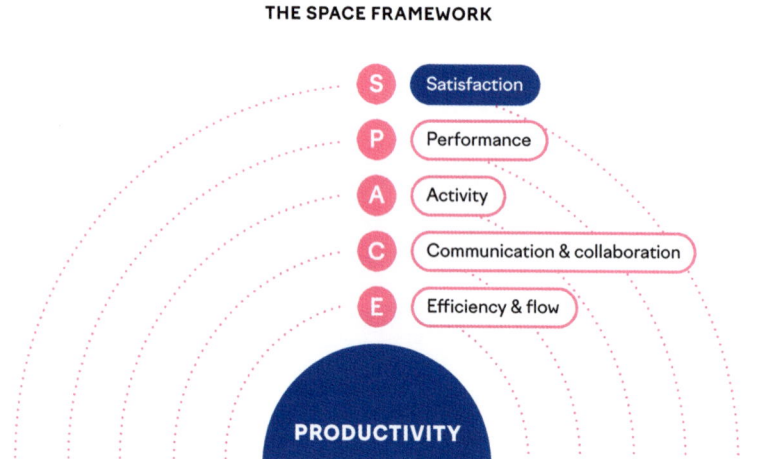

A set of universal metrics can't fully capture the effectiveness of your organization because organizations vary in size, age, and culture. A mature, larger organization may have very different challenges and therefore different areas to focus on for improvement compared to a smaller, newer organization. This means that while DORA metrics are incredibly useful, they must be complemented by other qualitative assessments, leadership insights, and perhaps more localized metrics that take into account the unique characteristics of specific teams.

Unfortunately, there is no definition of productivity that boils down to keeping an eye on a few simple metrics. Measuring productivity is actually pretty hard.

Measuring productivity

Engineering organizations measure developer productivity to eliminate bottlenecks and make data-informed decisions

> **Even when the intent of measuring productivity is to improve team and organizational effectiveness, individual engineers can still be concerned that the data will be used against them.**

about resource allocation and business objective alignment. Assessing productivity also provides insights into project predictability, which aids in planning and forecasting. This data acts as an early warning system to recognize when teams are overburdened, allowing for proactive interventions to alleviate stressors and redistribute workloads.

Even when the intent of measuring productivity is to improve team and organizational effectiveness, individual engineers can still be concerned that the data will be used against them. There's a pervasive worry that these metrics could translate into some form of individual performance review, even when that's not the intended use. This concern can contribute to a culture of apprehension, where engineers might be less willing to take risks, innovate, or openly discuss challenges. Any perception that the data will be weaponized for performance purposes can doom an effectiveness effort. Say that you won't use the data to target individuals and mean it.

Transparency in communicating the intent, scope, and limitations of productivity metrics can go a long way in assuaging these concerns. The metrics themselves likewise need to be transparent. By involving engineers in the process of deciding what to measure, how to measure it, and how the data will be used, you can mitigate fears and build a more cooperative culture focused on continuous improvement rather than punitive action.

Despite these risks, measuring productivity can foster healthy conversations about organizational improvement. Metrics can highlight inefficiencies or bottlenecks and open the door to constructive dialogue about how to solve these problems. This becomes especially necessary as a business grows and alignment between engineering objectives and broader business goals becomes more challenging. Software delivery metrics offer a standardized way to communicate the department's status to other organizational stakeholders.

Choose your metrics carefully. Besides the risk of impacting the psychological safety of your engineers, there are other pitfalls to be aware of. Don't rely on misleading or irrelevant metrics that provide a distorted view of what's happening within the teams (for example, pull requests per engineer or lines of code committed). Poorly chosen metrics can lead to misguided decisions and even undermine the credibility of the whole measurement process.

Consider, too, the incentives that are created when you choose metrics. Overemphasizing activity-focused numbers might lead engineers to game the system in a way that boosts activity metrics but doesn't genuinely improve their productivity or the value created by their work. This can result in a culture where superficial metrics are prized over substantive improvements, leading to technical debt and inefficiencies. On the other hand, if your metrics encourage engineers to submit more but smaller pull requests, you're likely to see benefits in quality and speed of delivery.

Cycle time

The work of delivering code changes for individual tasks is often measured in terms of cycle time. This term comes from manufacturing processes, where cycle time is the time it takes to produce a unit of product and lead time is the time it takes to fulfill a delivery request.

In software development, these terms are often mixed. For most features, it might not be reasonable to track the full lead time of a feature, as in the time from a customer requesting a feature to its delivery. Assuming the team is working on a product that's supposed to serve many customers, it's unrealistic to expect features to be shipped as soon as the team hears the idea.

Although we're reusing manufacturing terms, remember that there is no unit of product in software development. A car can only be sold by the manufacturer once. The work that happens in an engineering organization can be sold over and over again, with near-zero marginal cost for each additional sale of the exact same code.

When talking about cycle time for code, we're talking about the time it takes for code to reach production through development, reviews, and other process steps. Cycle time is the most important flow metric because it indicates how well your engine is running. When diagnosing a high cycle time, your team might have a conversation about topics like this:

- **What other things are we working on?** Start by visualizing all the work in progress. Be aware that your issue tracker might not tell the whole truth because development teams typically work on all kinds of ad hoc tasks.

- **How do we split our work?** It's generally a good idea to ship in small increments. This might be more difficult if you can't use feature flags to gradually roll out features to customers. Lack of infrastructure often leads to a bad branching strategy, with long-lived branches and additional coordination overhead.

- **What does our automated testing setup look like?** Is it easy to write and run tests? Can you trust the results from the continuous integration (CI) server?

- **How do we review code?** Is only one person in the team responsible for code reviews? Do you need to request reviews from an outside technology expert? Is it clear who's supposed to review code? Do we as a team value that work, or is someone pushing us to get back to coding?

- **How well do team members know the codebase?** If all the software was built by someone who left the company a while ago, chances are that development will be slow for a while.

- **Is there a separate testing/quality assurance stage?** Is testing happening close to the development team, or is the work handed off to someone on the outside?

- **How often do we deploy to production/release our software?** If test coverage is low, you might not feel like deploying on Fridays, or if deployment is not automated, you won't do it after every change. Deploying less frequently increases the batch size of a deployment, adding more risk and again reducing frequency.

- **How much time is spent on tasks beyond writing code?** Engineers need focus time; getting back to code on a 30-minute break between meetings is difficult.

There are perfectly good reasons for cycle time to fluctuate, and simply optimizing for a lower cycle time would be harmful. However, when used responsibly, it can be a great discussion starter. Even better, consider tools that help visualize how this number moves over time, leading to a deeper understanding of trends and causes.

Issue cycle time captures how long your epics, stories, and tasks (or however you plan your work) are in progress. Each team splits work differently, so they're not directly comparable. If you end up creating customer value, it probably doesn't matter whether that happens in five tasks taking four hours each or four tasks taking five hours each.

Things don't always go smoothly. When you expected something to take three days and it took four weeks of grinding, your team most likely missed an opportunity to adjust plans together. When you find yourself in this type of situation, here are some questions to ask.

- **What other things are we working on?** Chances are that your team delivered something, just not this feature. Visualizing work and limiting work in progress is a common cure.

- **How many people worked on this?** Gravitating toward solo projects might feel like it eliminates the communication overhead and helps move things faster, but this is only true from an individual's perspective, not the whole team's.

- **Are we good at sharing work?** Splitting work is both a personal skill and an organizational capability. Engineers will argue it's difficult to do. Nevertheless, do more of it, not less.

- **How accurate were our plans?** Suppose the scope of the feature increased by 200% during development. In that case, it's possible that you didn't understand the customer use cases, got surprised by the technical implementation, or simply discovered some nasty corner cases on the way.

- **Was it possible to split this feature into smaller but still functional slices?** Product management, product design, and engineers must work together to find a smart way to create the smallest possible end-to-end implementations. This is always difficult.

It feels great to work with a team that consistently delivers value to customers; that's what you get by improving issue cycle time.

Deployment frequency

Depending on the type of software you're building, "deployment" or "release" might mean different things. For a mobile app with an extensive QA process, getting to a two-week release cadence is already a good target, while the best teams building web backends deploy to production whenever a change is ready.

Deployment frequency serves as both a throughput and a quality metric. When a team is afraid to deploy, they'll do so less frequently. When they deploy less frequently, bigger deployment batches increase risk. Solving the problem typically requires building more infrastructure. Here are some of the main considerations:

- **If the build passes, can we feel good about deploying to production?** If not, you'll likely want to start building tests from the top of the pyramid to test for significant regressions, build the infrastructure for writing good tests, and ensure the team keeps writing tests for all new code. Whether tests get written cannot be dictated by outside stakeholders; this needs to be owned by the team.

- **If the build fails, do we know if it failed randomly or because of flaky tests?** You need to understand which tests are causing most of your headaches so that you can focus efforts on improving the situation.

- **Is the deployment pipeline to production fully automated?** If not, it's a good idea to keep automating it one step at a time. CI/CD pipeline investments start to pay off almost immediately.

- **Do we understand what happens in production after deployment?** Building observability and alerting takes time. If you have a good baseline setup, it's easy to keep adding these along with your regular development tasks. If you have nothing set up, it will never feel like it's the right time to add observability.

- **Are engineers educated on the production infrastructure?** Some engineers have never needed to touch a production environment. If it's not part of their onboarding, few people are courageous enough to start making improvements independently.

Some measures to avoid

Historically, agile teams have tracked velocity or story points. Originally meant as a way to help teams get better at splitting work and shipping value, these units have been abused ever since as a way to directly compare teams and steer an organization toward output-based thinking.

If talking about story points helps you be more disciplined about limiting queue depth and WIP, go for it. If not, don't feel bad about dropping story points as long as you understand your cycle times.

Another traditional management pitfall is to focus on utilization, thinking that you want your engineers to be 100% occupied. As utilization approaches 100%, cycle times shoot up and teams slow down. You'll also lose the ability to handle any reactive work that comes along without causing major disruptions to your other plans.

> The number of daily commits doesn't tell you anything about how good engineers are at their jobs.

There's a time and place to look at metrics around individual engineers. In very healthy environments, they can be used to improve the quality of coaching conversations while understanding the shortcomings of these measures. In a bigger organization, an effort to focus on individual metrics will likely derail your good intentions around data-driven continuous improvement. Engineers will rightfully point out how the number of daily commits doesn't tell you anything about how good they are at their jobs.

On the other hand, opportunities abound at the team level without shining a spotlight on any individual. Start your conversations there instead.

Classic productivity challenges

Assessing productivity challenges in software engineering teams requires looking beyond output metrics. Consider these potential culprits when trying to debug a productivity issue:

- **Insufficient collaboration.** Collaboration among team members is essential to improve issue cycle time. Collaboration allows for more effective planning and prioritization, reducing multitasking and aligning the team on common goals. Individual efforts may seem efficient in the short term, but they lack the collective intelligence and shared context that comes from teamwork.

- **Siloing.** To find gaps in collaboration, observe your issue tracker to see if projects are often completed by single contributors. A lack of multiple contributors on larger issues indicates a problem. Preventing siloing may involve setting team agreements and ensuring that tasks are broken down sufficiently for multiple people to work on.

- **Multitasking.** Taking on too many tasks simultaneously slows progress and creates waste. Track open stories, tasks, and epics against the number of engineers to gauge if there's an overload. Listen to the team's qualitative feedback on how they feel about their WIP levels. Introduce WIP limits to align everyone on completing existing tasks before starting new ones.

- **Large increments.** If projects often overrun, is the team trying to tackle overly large problems? Examine the time it takes to complete issues and look for scope creep to indicate planning deficiencies.

- **Planning quality.** When scope creep is common, consider it in future planning. You can also scrutinize long-running tasks to understand if they could have been broken down into smaller, more manageable parts, aiding in better planning for future issues.

- **Cross-team sequencing.** Even in the best-designed organizations, it's sometimes necessary for two teams to work together to deliver customer value. Without care and attention, these partnerships can struggle to stay coordinated and deliver the right thing at the right time for the other team to make progress.

It's worth mentioning that scope creep isn't necessarily a bad thing! Mitigating its effects should be focused on building in time for learning, feedback, and discovery; reducing scope creep via extensive up-front planning and specification rarely produces good results.

Setting goals around productivity

If you're just starting out on your productivity journey, goal-setting can feel intimidating, especially if you're trying to prove the value of investing in this area. It can be tempting to go straight to frameworks like DORA and SPACE and try to set goals around those concepts. Still, you'll have more luck if you identify a single opportunity from your conversations with engineers and execute on it (we'll talk more about this in the final chapter).

For example, if you learn that CI builds fail 20% of the time due to seemingly random environmental issues, that's a concrete data point to measure and set a target around. Once you hit the target, you can ensure you'll notice if you exceed it again. Rinse and repeat the process with different metrics for different kinds of improvements.

Once you've embraced that pattern, it's a good time to get DORA metrics in place if you haven't already and start using them to track the impact of improvements on teams and services. In many ways, the core DORA metrics cover the activity pillar in SPACE, and establishing them within your organization will quickly highlight potential opportunities.

As your productivity journey progresses, DORA metrics will continue to be useful for tracking trends, but they will never tell your whole productivity story. As you start to recognize themes in your work and your users' reported issues, embracing SPACE more thoroughly beyond the activity dimension will make sense. The SPACE framework is best used to identify various indicators of overall productivity, from OKR/goal attainment to meeting load to cross-team collaboration burden.

> Even under pressure, set goals around potential valuable outcomes from working on the problem, not on a restatement of the problem itself.

Setting goals around SPACE pillars is also fraught; there's no way, for example, to boil efficiency and flow down to a single number. On the other hand, SPACE is great as a framework to classify problems and brainstorm specific metrics you might use to track trends and validate improvements.

When it comes to setting metrics goals, you'll sometimes find yourself pressured to set a goal before you know how you're going to solve the fundamental problem. Even under pressure, set goals around potential valuable outcomes from working on the problem, not on a restatement of the problem itself.

Tools and tactics

Opportunities to improve flow exist throughout the reporting chain and sometimes straight up to senior leadership. Culturally, you need to get people at all levels to understand and internalize the idea that interruptions for software engineers are bad and should be minimized.

Of course, some interruptions are inevitable, but many are imposed without recognizing the cost. Before you do anything else with developer productivity, ensure there's general agreement on reducing interruptions (we'll discuss this in more detail in the next chapter).

At the team level, some interruptions are within the team's control and some are not. For example, suppose a code change requires a review from another team. In that case, the originating engineer is interrupted in their task until a person from the other team accepts the change, and the originating team may not feel in control of the situation in the meantime.

Nonetheless, plenty is in the control of individual teams: what they prioritize, how they work together, how they ensure quality, how they automate tedious tasks, and much more. Working agreements and retrospectives are two tools to use at the team level.

> Some interruptions are inevitable, but many are imposed without recognizing the cost.

Working agreement

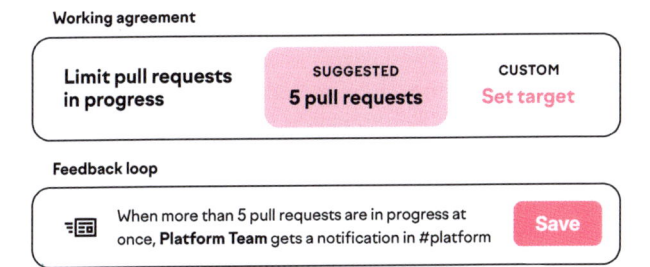

| Limit pull requests in progress | **SUGGESTED** 5 pull requests | **CUSTOM** Set target |

Feedback loop

When more than 5 pull requests are in progress at once, **Platform Team** gets a notification in #platform — Save

AN EXAMPLE WORKING AGREEMENT

- **Working agreements.** Team members agree on how they want to work. For example, team members could agree that they will release code at least once a day and that reviews should be completed within two hours of the assignment. By setting and monitoring these agreements, the team can recognize where they're falling short and identify resolutions that could be technical or process-focused.

- **Retrospectives.** Team members assess the work of the previous period, how they worked together, and how well they upheld the working agreements. They then propose ideas and accept action items for future iterations.

At the organizational level, we start to talk about more ambient interruptions, which no one is responsible for but just seem to appear. Tackling these interruptions is outside the scope of any one team unless a team is specifically responsible for this kind of thing. This is where things get more challenging but also more rewarding; solving these cross-team problems tends to have more leverage than focusing solely on team-level opportunities.

Once you reach a certain size, it's useful to be explicit about who is accountable for developer productivity and what it's like to build software at your company. If your immediate response is "everyone," either you are still a relatively small organization or it's time to start thinking about a more definitive answer.

What's next?

In this chapter, we discussed developer productivity, including ways to quantify it and guidance on goal-setting in the developer productivity space. Next, we'll talk about the less quantifiable but equally important developer experience.

FURTHER READING

The Principles of Product Development Flow: Second Generation Lean Product Development, by **Donald G. Reinertsen**. A comprehensive guide on applying lean principles to software and product development, enhancing productivity and efficiency.

The DevOps Handbook: How to Create World-Class Agility, Reliability, and Security in Technology Organizations, by **Gene Kim**, **Patrick Debois**, **John Willis**, and **Jez Humble**. Explains DevOps principles and practices, emphasizing collaboration and productivity in software development.

Making Work Visible: Exposing Time Theft to Optimize Work & Flow, by **Dominica DeGrandis**. Focuses on the importance of making work visible to improve productivity and efficiency in software development.

The Mythical Man-Month: Essays on Software Engineering, by **Frederick P. Brooks Jr.** A classic book in software engineering that discusses the challenges and pitfalls of managing complex software projects.

The SPACE of Developer Productivity, by **Nicole Forsgren** et al. The white paper that describes the SPACE framework and the multidimensional nature of "productivity."
queue.acm.org/detail.cfm?id=3454124

Build: Elements of an Effective
Software Organization

4. Developer Experience

Effective software organizations give engineers the support and tools they need to feel engaged.

In the previous chapter, we discussed how processes impact developer productivity and how we might measure it. Here, we look at the other side of software development: developer experience. We'll revisit the table stakes we discussed in previous chapters and explore the aspects of experience that we can measure and set goals around.

Measuring developer experience

Developer experience metrics are more qualitative than the metrics we saw in Chapter 3. For example, it's table stakes to capture employee satisfaction and engagement data. Still, you'd be hard-pressed to suggest that this is quantitative data; the small number of data points makes the error bars quite wide.

Suppose you want to understand how developer experience affects your team's effectiveness. In that case, you need to evaluate how employees feel about their work and other factors contributing to overall job satisfaction, examining the following points:

- **Sources of frustration.** Software engineers get frustrated when their flow is interrupted — sometimes by a tool, sometimes by a process, and sometimes by another human. These frustrations add up, impacting the engineer's sense of satisfaction at getting things done while also working against timely delivery. Consider making it easy and obvious to report engineer frustrations to a ticket queue that you check regularly.

- **Employee satisfaction and engagement.** This measures how content and committed employees are. Regular employee surveys can help capture this data.

Additionally, exit interviews and employee reviews on job websites can offer insightful perspectives on employee satisfaction and engagement.

- **Employee turnover and regretted attrition.** Employee turnover refers to the rate at which employees leave an organization. A high turnover rate, especially among high-performing or recently hired individuals, could indicate underlying organizational issues. An increase in regretted attrition — the loss of employees that the organization would have preferred to retain — is a warning sign of poor organizational health.

- **Leadership trust and communication effectiveness.** Leadership and organizational communication effectiveness can significantly impact employee satisfaction. Regular surveys can gauge employees' trust in leadership and the effectiveness of organization-wide communications, providing insight into potential areas for improvement in leadership and communication strategies.

Note that a couple of downsides plague each of these metrics: the data arrives long after the damage is done, and the data is noisy and nuanced.

Identifying improvements

The people whose productivity you are trying to improve are the best source of information about what needs improving. You can better understand their needs by approaching this on two fronts: talking to the users of your internal development systems and collecting data about tool behavior as engineers go about their day.

Review the table stakes

We discussed organization-wide table stakes in Chapter 1 (empowered teams, rapid feedback, and outcomes over outputs), and we discussed team-specific table stakes in Chapter 3 (limited queue depth, small batch sizes, limited work in progress).

All of these come into play in developer experience. The absence of any one of these is known to reduce a software engineer's satisfaction and engagement with the job.

As a leader, you need to honestly evaluate where your team and/or organization stands regarding this must-have list. If any of these ways of working are missing or on shaky ground, you (and your leadership) must acknowledge that there's a ceiling on the improvements you can make until that changes.

Talk to your users

The phrase "talk to your users" may be unexpected here, but it's a surprisingly helpful framing. Your engineering colleagues are your users, and your product is effectiveness. As with the real-world users of your company's product, talking to your internal users can be a source of powerful insights. This can take a few forms.

Have as many in-person conversations with small groups of engineers — including both veterans and new hires, product and platform teams — as you can manage. You could do this via a survey, but have at least some of these conversations in person with a few teams; that environment tends to generate usefully divergent ideas.

YOU CAN USE PROMPTS LIKE THESE:

- What could we improve about your tools?
- What's an annoyance for engineers today that could become a real risk in the future?
- What would help the company learn more quickly through rapid feedback?

If you've established a high-trust environment, go a step further and shadow engineers while they do their job. You'll be amazed at the workarounds you never knew people were employing and the things you didn't realize people were putting up with.

Many or even most of the ideas you'll come across will have technical solutions, but don't tune out people, processes, and political challenges that merit different approaches. Increasing engineering leverage without spending engineering time could be a huge win.

Collect empirical data

Your users will suggest lots of opportunities for improvement — so many, in fact, that you'll have difficulty choosing from among them, and the initial list will feel infinite. This is when it's essential to have quantitative data to help guide your prioritization and validate the qualitative stories you hear. Be honest about what you can, can't, will, and won't do.

It's relatively easy to build observability into your internal tooling. If you don't already have a system to record the behavior of internal tools, now might be the time to consider buying or building one. An internal tool should be able to record every invocation and its outcome, along with various metadata about the interaction. Most importantly, it should record how long a developer has waited to get output from the tool.

If you make it easy to capture user experience data from internal tools — say, by providing a standard API that other engineers can use to collect signals that can be stored usefully alongside other tooling data — internal tool authors will tend to capture some metrics.

> **An internal tool should be able to record every invocation and its outcome, along with various metadata about the interaction.**

Developer surveys

Surveys are integral tools for comprehending developer experience beyond the team level. They provide two kinds of value:

- **Validation.** Surveys act as a barometer, gauging whether the organization's strategies, tools, and policies align with its intended outcomes. Essentially, they confirm whether you're on the right path toward improving the developer experience.

- **Discovery.** Beyond mere validation, surveys also function as windows into the uncharted territories of developer needs, wants, and challenges. They help organizations discover fresh avenues for improvement.

HOW TO USE SURVEYS

It's good to do a comprehensive developer survey once or twice a year, plus more informal but more frequent surveys with smaller audiences. Here are a few statements that we've found particularly useful to evaluate:

- I feel safe expressing concerns to my team.
- My team makes frequent improvements based on feedback.
- My team systematically validates user needs.
- I have enough uninterrupted time for focus work.
- It's simple to make changes to the codebases I work with.

Ask about a timeframe short enough to remember but long enough to be representative: "the last month" or "the last week," but probably not "the last six months." Clearly defining the period reduces random bias from people's interpretations and assumptions. With that in mind, avoid questions and prompts that include "since the last survey," as well as those that ask how or whether something has improved over an indefinite timeframe. Use past survey data to assess changes over time (and recognize that fully rolling out a survey question will take at least two rounds).

You can make the responses fully open to promote transparency and discussion, or you can run a confidential survey to lower the threshold for reporting problems. Either way, explicitly clarify how the responses will be used and reported. If you go with confidential surveys, you need to be mindful of a few key points:

- **Limit access to identifying data.** For example, a breakdown of survey results by tenure can be extremely identifying in a small-ish company that's been around for a while.

- **If you say the responses are anonymous, mean it.** Make it impossible to link a response back to a person or any identifying metadata.

- **Anonymous doesn't mean unpublished.** Make clear to survey respondents whether you will publish unattributed commentary.

THE CHALLENGES OF SURVEYS

One of the primary issues you'll run into with surveys is the squeaky wheel syndrome, where the loudest voices overshadow more valuable feedback. In this situation, you could inadvertently channel resources to appease this vocal subset, neglecting the broader (and sometimes more pertinent) issues. Another challenge is recency bias, where respondents predominantly focus on recent events while filling out the survey, leaving behind older yet still impactful concerns. This bias can sometimes amplify the significance of recent minor issues while diminishing long-standing critical ones.

Sampling bias further complicates the survey landscape. Without meticulous design and execution, surveys might inadvertently cater to a specific developer subset. You might end up with feedback that doesn't holistically represent the sentiments of the entire organization. Your best way to avoid this bias is to encourage participation at a level close to 100% of the engineering organization.

THE CHALLENGES OF SURVEYS

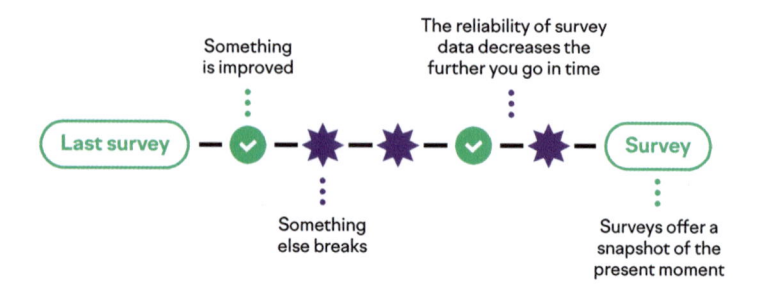

Diagram: A timeline from "Last survey" to "Survey" with events in between—"Something is improved," "Something else breaks," "The reliability of survey data decreases the further you go in time," and "Surveys offer a snapshot of the present moment."

Then there's the challenge of striking the right frequency. If you deploy surveys too often, you may run into survey fatigue, diminishing the quality and quantity of feedback. However, sparse surveys can fail to capture rapidly evolving sentiments.

There's also an inherent risk in tying objectives too tightly to survey outcomes. While responding to feedback is vital, it's equally important to recognize that surveys are but one facet of a multi-dimensional landscape. Over-reliance can lead to reactive strategies rather than proactive ones.

DIVERSIFYING FEEDBACK CHANNELS

While surveys provide valuable insights, diversifying feedback channels ensures a richer, more rounded understanding of developer experience. Regular one-on-one sessions, open discussions, a forum for submitting frustrations, shadowing sessions, or even casual coffee chats can offer more continuous insights into developer sentiments. Telemetry can also provide continuous, passive feedback on tool usage patterns and potential pain points.

Fighting back against interruptions

One of the critical concepts in productivity is flow, as represented by the efficiency and flow pillar of SPACE. Uninterrupted time is the building block of flow; in most organizations, there tend to be plenty of interruptions to measure. These come in all shapes and sizes, from meetings to GitHub outages and everything in between. Some interruptions are more negatively impactful than others, especially in aggregate. The right metrics for your purposes will depend on how you understand the nature of the productivity challenges in your organization.

Interruptions — anything that yanks a developer out of that elusive flow state — can appear out of nowhere. They're often untracked and underestimated in their ability to derail focus and productivity.

Some interruptions are genuinely urgent and require immediate attention. Others stem from outdated processes or habits and can be scheduled for later. An approach based on

INTERRUPTIONS

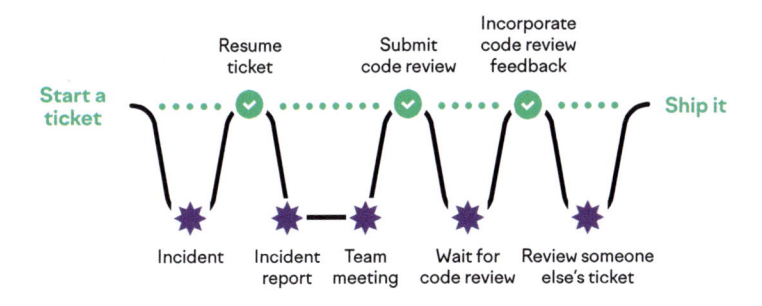

THE EISENHOWER MATRIX

	Urgent	Not urgent
Important	Crying baby Kitchen fire Some calls **1**	Exercise Vocation Planning **2**
Not important	**3** Interruptions Distractions Other calls	**4** Trivia Busy work Time wasters

the Eisenhower matrix can involve categorizing interruptions based on urgency and impact and then devising a strategy to handle each category effectively.

1. **Urgent and important.** Issues like production outages that demand immediate attention and generally have team-wide consensus for prioritization. Certain customer situations can also fall into this category.

2. **Important but not urgent.** Things like discussing plans for a new feature are important, but not necessarily time-sensitive.

3. **Urgent but unimportant.** This is the class of interruptions that an engineer could solve but an equally good and more timely response is available elsewhere. For example, this kind of interruption happens when a junior engineer asks a senior to answer a blocking question, even though the answer is well-documented and was also answered via chat last week.

④ Neither urgent nor important. Questions or issues that could have waited or been solved through other means. These are especially disruptive because they often don't warrant the break in focus they cause. For example, this can happen when a manager stops by an engineer's desk without recognizing that the engineer is otherwise focused.

Certain types of interruptions require a broader organizational fix rather than individual adjustments — interruptions like meetings, internal support, external support, and production incidents. These not only impact the effectiveness of individual software developers but can also destabilize teams and processes as a whole, especially as a company scales.

The meeting dilemma

Meetings within an organization exhibit a wide range of effectiveness. Some prove to be instrumental in decision-making and collaboration, while others can frankly be worthless (and occasionally verging on harmful). The underlying cost of a meeting isn't limited to its duration; it extends to the interruption of deep focus and to the trust that the meeting either creates or erodes.

Engineers should designate blocks of time for focused work, and these should remain inviolate. Calendar features like auto-decline can safeguard these precious hours, preserving dedicated work time.

> **A universal objective should be to secure uninterrupted blocks of concentration for all roles.**

The frequency of meetings often correlates with job responsibilities. Leadership roles, such as engineering managers and tech leads, may find their schedules more populated with meetings than other team members. Despite this variance, a universal objective should be to secure uninterrupted blocks of concentration for all roles. For example, among ICs, you could aim for at least four hours of focused work on four days each week.

Minimizing and optimizing meetings frees up significant blocks of productive time for teams. Here are some effective strategies to consider:

- **Clear objectives.** Before scheduling a meeting, clarify its purpose. If the objective can be achieved through an email or a quick chat, opt for that instead.

- **Audit recurring meetings.** Periodically review standing meetings to determine if they're still relevant or if their frequency can be reduced. Some weekly meetings might be just as effective if held bi-weekly or monthly.

- **Agenda requirement.** Insist on an agenda for every meeting. This ensures that the meeting stays on track and can also help participants evaluate if their attendance is essential.

- **Time limits.** Meetings that exceed 30 minutes should be rare, and meetings that exceed an hour should be exceptional. Even for large undertakings, long meetings tend to hurt more than they help. Conversely, a series of shorter meetings, with time to reflect on each, is more likely to result in powerful outcomes.

- **Limit attendees.** Invite only those who are essential to the meeting's objective. A smaller, more relevant group can often make decisions more quickly.

- **Share the outcome of meetings.** Small, focused, agenda-driven meetings don't need to be secretive. Create a mailing list or chat channel where people can stay up to date on projects or meetings they're interested in without having to attend all the time or feel like they're missing out.

- **Empowered decision-making.** Establish clear protocols for decision-making that don't always rely on group consensus. Empower individuals or smaller teams to make decisions where appropriate.

- **Asynchronous updates.** For meetings that are informational or offer updates, consider asynchronous methods. This could be recorded video updates or written reports (or both) that individuals can review independently. Remember that you'll frequently need to provide the same message multiple times in multiple ways, so if it's important — like an all-hands meeting — make a point of ensuring that people receive and incorporate the information.

A note on asynchronous collaboration

Asynchronous collaboration offers a significant advantage over certain in-person meetings: it allows engineers to choose when to engage with a task rather than disrupt their focus for a meeting at a potentially inconvenient time. It also alleviates the need to cram knowledge work into a 30-minute timeslot.

To be successful at working asynchronously on decisions, it's useful to specifically define how you'll handle them. One practical step is to create templates for common decision-making processes. These templates provide a structured approach to things like:

- **Design reviews.** A document to propose designs for a significant new feature or capability. It describes the business need, explains non-goals and tradeoffs, and solicits feedback on key decisions.

- **Build vs. buy decisions.** A document to capture the pros and cons of building a solution in-house versus purchasing an off-the-shelf solution.

- **New API or common library designs.** A document detailing the requirements, expected benefits, and potential impacts of introducing a new API or shared library.

Shared documents become a central part of asynchronous collaboration. They allow team members to add their input, edit, and comment in real time or at their convenience. Establishing a window of time for commenting — a set period during which team members can review and provide feedback — ensures that discussions are timely but not rushed.

While the goal is to minimize live meetings, some topics may still require synchronous communication to move the conversation forward. A meeting is valid in this case, but think carefully about who needs to be there. To make it easy for people to consume the meeting without attending, record the meeting and designate someone to take notes.

The effectiveness of asynchronous collaboration depends on the tools at hand. Even today, some mainstream tools fall far short of supporting collaborative asynchronous work. Invest in tools that enable real-time editing, commenting, and sharing.

While asynchronous collaboration is powerful, there are also times when a quick synchronous discussion is more effective. Providing the means to effortlessly transition to an audio or video call, or the physical space to have a quick conversation, can resolve complex issues more quickly.

Internal support

Internal support in a software organization ensures the smooth functioning of teams, particularly as software engineers assist their peers in navigating and completing tasks. It acts as a bridge, filling in knowledge gaps, clarifying doubts, and facilitating better understanding. As vital as it is, this very support system is typically disorganized, ad hoc, unrecognized, and itself unsupported — for example, a single developer support channel in a messaging tool where everyone asks everything. As such, it can become a significant source of interruptions, especially when the demand surpasses the supply of knowledgeable peers who can assist.

One common cause of increased demand for internal support is the absence of self-serve solutions. In an ideal scenario, engineers would have tools, platforms, and documentation at their disposal to independently find answers to their queries. Without these, they're left with no choice but to seek help from others, leading to frequent interruptions for both the one seeking help and the one providing it. Similarly, when clear, straightforward processes (aka happy paths) for common tasks aren't established, engineers often find themselves in a labyrinth of trial and error, pulling in colleagues to help navigate.

> **When knowledge becomes the domain of a select few and isn't disseminated broadly, it creates an environment where constant queries become the norm.**

Perhaps more insidious is the issue of knowledge siloing. When knowledge becomes the domain of a select few and isn't disseminated broadly, it creates an environment where constant queries become the norm. Those in the know are frequently interrupted, and those out of the loop continually seek guidance. If a subset of engineers always provides support, it may prevent others from developing problem-solving skills and self-sufficiency. You can solve this through knowledge-sharing sessions, shadowing sessions, and partnering on tasks unfamiliar to other team members.

However, relying heavily on certain team members can stifle growth opportunities for the wider team. Similarly, if only a few individuals are leaned on for support continuously, it may lead to a scenario where critical knowledge resides with only those few. This creates vulnerability in the team dynamics if these individuals are unavailable. As a leader, you need to make sure those people make a point of taking real time away from work so that the organization can see how it reacts.

While internal support is an invaluable aspect of work in software organizations, without the right structures and resources in place, it can morph from a support system into a persistent source of disruptions for a small group of people who could be producing a lot more value. AI search tools and knowledge-sharing sessions can help fill the gap, while collaborative ways of working can help it from showing up in the first place.

External support

External support, especially for customers, users, and user-facing colleagues, comes with its own set of challenges. The requests can be unpredictable, of varying quality, and cover a broad spectrum of topics. Some may be straightforward and easy to address, while others might be vague, complex, or even misdirected, requiring more time and effort to resolve.

To manage these sorts of demands, tools and processes like ticket queues and WIP limits are invaluable. Here's why.

- **Visibility.** Ticket queues provide a clear view of incoming requests, shedding light on the current workload and types of issues being raised.

- **Prioritization.** Understanding the queue helps in resource allocation. It becomes feasible to triage requests, ensuring that high-priority or urgent issues are addressed swiftly and engineers are only pulled in when necessary.

- **Workload management.** WIP limits act as a buffer, ensuring that support teams aren't swamped with an unmanageable number of requests at once. This allows for a consistent quality of support.

To further streamline the process, office hours can be a big help. Setting specific periods dedicated to addressing external queries ensures:

- **Predictability.** Both the support team and those seeking support have a defined window. This clarity helps in setting expectations.

- **Focus.** When not in the office hours window, teams can redirect their attention to other pressing tasks, ensuring a balanced distribution of effort and time.

Continually analyze your support workload to find things you could proactively address. Self-serve configuration, UX improvements, help center articles, guides, or training sessions can completely eliminate entire categories of customer support requests.

Production incidents

Just as all meetings aren't created equal, the same goes for incidents. When assessing incidents, several factors matter.

- **Frequency.** How often are incidents happening?
- **Severity.** How significant is the problem — is it a minor hiccup or a full-blown outage?
- **Impact.** What were the broader consequences for systems and users?
- **Time spent.** How long did the incident last? How much time did we spend on it after that?

If you're tracking these parameters, do so transparently. Incident metrics should inform, not intimidate, ensuring that no one feels the need to underreport or diminish the scale of an incident.

Truly blameless post-incident reviews can be transformative, providing a platform to dissect what went wrong and how to prevent future occurrences. By identifying patterns and drawing up actionable items from each incident, teams are better poised to anticipate and mitigate future challenges.

Moreover, integrating tools for incident analysis can offer granular insights, highlighting potential areas of vulnerability. Implementing a first-responder rotation ensures that a dedicated team is always on standby, primed to tackle incidents, and can distribute responsibility more evenly.

> **By identifying patterns and drawing up actionable items from each incident, teams are better poised to anticipate and mitigate future challenges.**

Are you interruption-aware?

Answering the following questions can reveal insights into how well the organization is prepared to manage interruptions. The goal isn't to eliminate them entirely but rather to measure, reduce, and manage them in a way that aligns with the team's needs and the organization's objectives.

1. **Do you have a system for tracking interruptions?** Understanding the nature and urgency of interruptions can go a long way in managing them effectively. Are you capturing data on what kinds of interruptions are most frequent and which types disproportionately affect certain team members? This will help in deciding where to invest time in process improvements.

2. **Are you measuring the right things?** Metrics offer a quantitative way to understand the burden of interruptions, but are you measuring the things that truly matter? For instance, beyond just

tracking the number of meetings, are we looking at their ROI? And when it comes to internal and external support, do you have visibility into how much time is spent and the quality of those interactions?

3. **How much slack do teams have?** If you aim for 100% utilization, you're setting yourself up for failure. What level of buffer time do you build into our sprints or roadmaps to account for inevitable interruptions, and are you revisiting these assumptions periodically to ensure they still hold?

4. **How do you capture and share knowledge?** Many interruptions, especially internal support ones, can be reduced through better knowledge sharing. Do you have a centralized repository, internal forums, or other mechanisms where team members can find answers to common questions? How often is this resource updated, and is it easily accessible to everyone?

5. **Are there more things you could automate or make self-serve?** Many interruptions stem from the fact that it's never seemed worthwhile to automate something or make it self-serve for a non-engineer — it seems easier to just have an engineer do it when it needs doing. If you feel like interruptions are getting in your way, that mindset might not be helping. Automate the things that are pulling your engineers' attention away from their work.

The dynamics of interruptions will change significantly as a company grows and its needs change. By taking an ongoing and proactive approach to these interruptions, software engineering organizations can build more sustainable, efficient, and resilient work environments. When you make your processes interruption-aware, your team can focus on what they do best: building great products.

Setting experience goals

When you get specific about the source of interruptions that prevent continuous focus, you have something more satisfying than just satisfaction surveys: metrics that can be measured reliably and consistently, and thus, metrics we can seek to improve. That doesn't mean you throw out the satisfaction survey; you just accept it as a lagging indicator as you improve the things above. Satisfaction is a measurement you use to validate your work, not something you try to chase week to week.

> **Tracking bad days across the engineering organization provides insights into common pain points and opportunities for improvement.**

User experience objectives (UXOs) offer a complementary framework for thinking about developer experience. With UXOs, you agree on acceptable behavior for your tools. As a few very basic examples, you can agree that `git pull` should never take more than two minutes, saving in an editor should rarely take more than two seconds, and CI/CD checks should return results within 15 minutes.

These UXOs can operate independently, guiding experience goals for individual tools. Their potency increases when aggregated. When a developer experiences breaches in a certain number of UXOs, you know that the developer is having a bad day. Tracking bad days across the engineering organization provides insights into common pain points and opportunities for improvement.

UXOs also furnish real-time insights into engineers' experiences, allowing for adaptable goal-setting and innovative problem-solving. Setting goals around UXOs versus completing a specific project or task lets you work to improve developer experience without being constrained by rigid plans.

Don't confuse UXOs with service-level objectives (SLOs), as unlike SLO breaches, UXO breaches aren't necessarily urgent; they define expectations for tool behavior that the user can measure their experience against, which can guide a tooling team on where to spend its time.

UXOs focus on meaningful enhancements, fostering a direct connection between the lived experiences of engineers and the people responsible for supporting those experiences. They fill the gap when you're tempted to set goals based on surveys or other sources of organizational health metrics.

Just because you're not setting goals for these metrics doesn't mean that you shouldn't know what "good" would look like in your organization. Getting to 100% satisfaction or zero regretted attrition is unrealistic, so what would your organization consider success? There's likely to be a ceiling on overall satisfaction and a floor on regretted attrition, both put in place by your organization's culture and incentive structure.

What's next?

In this chapter, we looked at developer experience and the things that influence it, focusing especially on different types of interruptions and mitigations. We wrestled with the fact that most developer experience data will be qualitative and that many developer experience problems require non-code solutions and explored options to set developer experience goals.

In the next chapter, we'll look at how to put the lessons of this and previous chapters into practice. ✸

FURTHER READING

Drive: The Surprising Truth About What Motivates Us, by **Daniel H. Pink**. Explores the core elements of motivation and how they can be applied in a work environment, including for software developers.

Flow: The Psychology of Optimal Experience, by **Mihaly Csikszentmihalyi**. Discusses in detail how uninterrupted focus allows people to reach a state of heightened efficiency and satisfaction in their work.

Peopleware: Productive Projects and Teams, by **Tom DeMarco** and **Timothy Lister**. A classic in the software development field, focusing on the human side of software development and team dynamics.

Deep Work: Rules for Focused Success in a Distracted World, by **Cal Newport**. A guide on how to achieve focused and productive work, which is particularly relevant for developers dealing with complex tasks and needing deep focus.

Agile Retrospectives: Making Good Teams Great, by **Esther Derby** and **Diana Larsen**. Provides tools and techniques for effective agile retrospectives, emphasizing continuous improvement and problem-solving throughout a project's life.

Site Reliability Engineering: How Google Runs Production Systems, by **Niall Richard Murphy**, **Betsy Beyer**, **Chris Jones**, and **Jennifer Petoff**. An in-depth look into Google's approach to building, deploying, monitoring, and maintaining some of the largest software systems in the world, including incident management processes.

The Field Guide to Understanding "Human Error", by **Sidney Dekker**. While not exclusively about software engineering, this book is highly regarded in the Learning From Incidents community. It offers insights into how to understand and learn from human errors in complex systems.

Build: Elements of an Effective Software Organization

5. Putting It All Together

Now it's time to take everything you've read and turn it into a plan. Your company's size, age, and culture guarantee that your situation is unique, so we're limited in making hyper-specific recommendations. Still, there are some proven patterns in structuring any organization for success, rolling out an effectiveness effort, and choosing and monitoring metrics.

In this chapter, we'll share our experience with the foundational work of identifying and eliminating bottlenecks at the team level. Then, we'll outline a high-level framework for implementing an organization-wide effectiveness effort. We'll wrap up by talking about the challenges of managing change and sharing a framework for managing change-related feelings.

Identifying and eliminating delivery bottlenecks

At Swarmia, we've seen time and again that when teams focus on improving just a few key areas, the payoff comes quickly.

- **Workflow.** What does the flow of work look like for your team? Does everything take forever, or do things normally go fine, with the exception of some worrisome outliers? Do you routinely finish the things you start? How much time does work spend in a waiting state?

- **Priorities & WIP limits.** Does your team have clear, stable priorities? How many things does your team work on at once? Is it generally obvious to software engineers what they should work on next? Do you feel like your team is too busy to ever do anything well?

- **Keeping the lights on (KTLO).** How much time does your team spend doing chores or fighting fires due to past decisions? How does this affect your ability to deliver predictably? How does it impact morale?

- **Manual work and toil.** What does the team do manually on a somewhat predictable basis and why? Are your tests, deployments, and rollbacks all automated? Does your team planning include time to automate these tasks regularly?

- **Decisions owned outside the team.** How often does the team need to wait on someone on the outside to make progress with their work?

Here's a closer look at each area, what it looks like when you have bottlenecks, and what to start doing *today* to get things on a better path.

WORKFLOW

What to watch for

- Consistent delays in task completion.
- Certain types of tasks are routinely blocked.
- Unpredictable delivery.

What to start doing today

- Track cycle times and change lead times for your code changes and issues (task, story, epic, bug, etc.)
- Track the time engineers spend waiting on CI/CD.
- Track the time work is waiting or idle.

PRIORITIES & WIP LIMITS

What to watch for

- More work in progress than members on the team.
- Overwhelmed engineers.
- Frequent changes in priorities.
- Unfinished work.

What to start doing today

- Set a WIP limit for roadmap projects/stories, starting with the number of devs in the team divided by 2.
- Learn how to collaborate and plan work in a way that allows multiple engineers to work on a larger roadmap item.
- Only allow a higher WIP limit when workflow metrics are not ballooning because of the change.
- Maintaining some "slack" in your capacity increases your ability to deliver faster. Aim for 75-85% utilization of your team (not 100%) to preserve the team's productivity.

KTLO & REACTIVE WORK

What to watch for

- KTLO consumes more than 30% of a team's time.
- Incidents cause frequent disruptions to focused work.
- Team goals are routinely delayed due to lack of slack to handle reactive work.

What to start doing today

- Track change failure rate to understand quality.
- Track engineering investment according to the Balance Framework, explained in Chapter 2.
- If a team is spending more than 30% of its capacity on KTLO and reactive work, consider whether this could be reduced by prioritizing work that improves quality, customer support (discussed in Chapter 4), or developer productivity. If prioritizing that work isn't practical, consider whether the team is the right size for the surface it owns.

MANUAL WORK AND TOIL

What to watch for

- Recurring manual tasks are time-consuming and error-prone.
- Deployments require human attention.

What to start doing today

- Automate CI/CD and deployments.
- Create a culture where quick automations just get done without extensive discussion.
- Check your investment balance to make sure you always invest at least 10% of your capacity in productivity improvements.
- Encourage and incentivize conversations about productivity improvements.

> **DECISIONS OWNED OUTSIDE THE TEAM**
>
> **What to watch for**
>
> - Work stalls while waiting for external input.
> - Poor sequencing of dependencies.
> - Top-down priority changes.
>
> **What to start doing today**
>
> - Consider the guidance in Chapter 2 about organizing teams and making tradeoffs. Are the tradeoffs you made still the right ones?
> - Ensure your team has the skills it needs to operate effectively without requiring regular technical assistance.
> - Quantify the impact of processes that are external to your team in terms of wait time, effort, and interruptions.
> - Establish visibility into the progress of cross-team initiatives.

Finding opportunities in these areas is usually painfully straightforward, and chances are good that engineers in your organization already have strong ideas about what to do. Acting on those opportunities will require finding ways to invest in the time and culture needed to implement solutions now and moving forward.

Convenient fallacies to avoid

Certain fallacies tend to come up whenever people talk about bottlenecks. In the course of your conversations, it will be tempting for you or someone else to say things like:

Putting It All Together

- **"We aren't doing enough up-front requirement-gathering."** Detailed up-front requirements aren't just unnecessary — they can be detrimental when they restrict a team's ability to adapt and evolve as projects progress. The most successful projects embrace evolving requirements, allowing for innovation and responsive changes. Adhering too rigidly to initial specifications leads to inefficiency and stifles innovative solutions.

- **"What we really need is more people."** The notion that insufficient staffing is a primary bottleneck overlooks the underlying issue of WIP limits. Adding more staff to a project does not solve productivity problems; it often exacerbates them due to onboarding costs and increased coordination challenges. Effective productivity stems from ruthless prioritization and managing and optimizing the workload and capabilities of the existing team, not indiscriminately increasing team size.

- **"We just need to plan better."** Extensive planning is often mistakenly idolized as the key to successful project execution. Over-planning can bind a team to a trajectory that may become irrelevant as project dynamics evolve. Effective planning requires balance — it provides direction, but not so much that it impedes flexibility and rapid response to change.

- **"It doesn't work that way here."** Perhaps when you hear this, you'll have stumbled upon the exact problem, but it's not one you can solve with code. Culture change might be needed to embrace all the recommendations in this book, and culture change is scary and hard.

Generally, be wary of claims that more processes will make things go faster, and be skeptical when someone suggests a headcount fix (unless they're advocating for staffing a platform team, that is). Remember, any proposed fix that changes the size, shape, or remit of a team can affect productivity — positively or negatively — for months.

Keep effectiveness top of mind

An effective engineering organization is a differentiator in recruiting and retaining engineers and bringing value to your users. Engineering effectiveness should be an ongoing top-of-mind concern because it's an engineering organization's single best lever for delivering more and better business results.

Encourage your team to experiment with new methods, tools, and processes. WIP limits are especially interesting to experiment with if you haven't done so before. Create an environment where process experimentation is allowed and part of the team's culture. Whether it's adopting new software tools or implementing automation, these experiments can lead to significant productivity gains.

Embed continuous improvement into your team's routine. Regularly discuss topics like workflow, priority management, and automation opportunities. This keeps the team focused on productivity and encourages a culture of ongoing improvement. Use these discussions not only to identify areas for improvement but also to plan and commit to specific actions. Keep the focus on the team's way of working, not on any individual.

Involve business stakeholders in your improvement initiatives. Their understanding and support can be pivotal, especially when changes impact timelines or require resources. Demonstrate with data that the proposed changes align with business goals, and lean on "the business" to support you with time, tooling, and training. Yes, this could be hard, but improvements in this space don't come for free in the short term, even while they pay for themselves in the long term.

Alternatively, don't involve business stakeholders if your reality doesn't allow for it. You can make improvements just within your group team, without support from the organization or the business, but you may need to get creative in the short term. In the long term, demonstrated improvement might buy you the agency to make bigger changes with bigger results — or give you a great story to tell when you start looking for a new role.

> **Engineering effectiveness is an engineering organization's single best lever for delivering more and better business results.**

Implement and track metrics that accurately reflect the team's improvement over time. This could include tracking DORA, SPACE, or other relevant metrics. Regularly review these metrics to assess whether your changes are working. This data-driven approach not only helps to fine-tune your tactics but also provides tangible evidence of improvement, which can be motivating for the team and reassuring for stakeholders.

Know when to move on

As one bottleneck is addressed and resolved, it ceases to be the limiting factor in your workflow. The new bottleneck is in another area of the process. At this point, it's time to move from actively working on the first bottleneck toward monitoring it to ensure there's no backsliding.

By continuously moving the focus to the current bottleneck, you maintain a steady flow in your processes, enhancing overall efficiency and productivity. Identifying, addressing, and monitoring bottlenecks is an ongoing process — one part of an overall effort at continuous improvement.

Driving an effectiveness effort

Implementing an engineering effectiveness program is no small feat, and thoughtfully sequencing your approach will increase your chances of success. Here, we sketch a roadmap to guide you on this journey, broken down into six key stages: ❶ **baseline**, ❷ **research**, ❸ **act**, ❹ **invest**, ❺ **normalize**, and ❻ **sustain** (or BRAINS, for a memorable acronym):

❶ In the **baseline** stage, you lay the groundwork for your journey. Start with an inventory of the metrics you have today. Implement tooling and processes to understand the current delivery and team health situation.

❷ Next, immerse yourself in the environment of your engineering teams during the **research** stage, seeking to understand their challenges and victories first-hand through shadowing, interviews, and hands-on work.

❸ With this understanding, **act** immediately to implement small but meaningful improvements that can positively impact the team's work.

❹ After tackling quick wins, it's time to **invest** in longer-term improvements. Start standardizing processes and tools across teams to reduce complexity and improve consistency.

Putting It All Together

5 Having implemented these changes, you can work to **normalize** the new processes across the organization, increasing adoption to maximize impact.

6 Finally, commit to long-term investments in improving the developer experience in the **sustain** stage. The challenges you face will evolve as the company itself does.

1 BASELINE

The first step is understanding your current situation.

Start from the table stakes identified in Chapter 1 (for organizations) and Chapter 3 (for teams). Does your organization uphold and support these table stakes? If not, as mentioned earlier, there will be a ceiling on the improvement you can achieve.

Take an inventory of the delivery-related metrics you have today and identify useful ones that would be easy to add. Take a moment to assess team health by considering satisfaction, attrition rates, and engagement levels. If you're still small, this should happen organically; once you're larger than 10 engineers, you may also want to create more intentional feedback mechanisms. Paint a picture of where things stand today for yourself and your stakeholders.

This is also a good time to consider implementing DORA metrics that accurately represent your software delivery performance. Getting these metrics in place demands developing a discipline (and systems) that you'll be grateful for in the future.

Now is also a good time to routinely attach Balance Framework labels to your work items to start to paint a picture of where your time is going. You may want to build or buy a

Putting It All Together

THE BRAINS FRAMEWORK

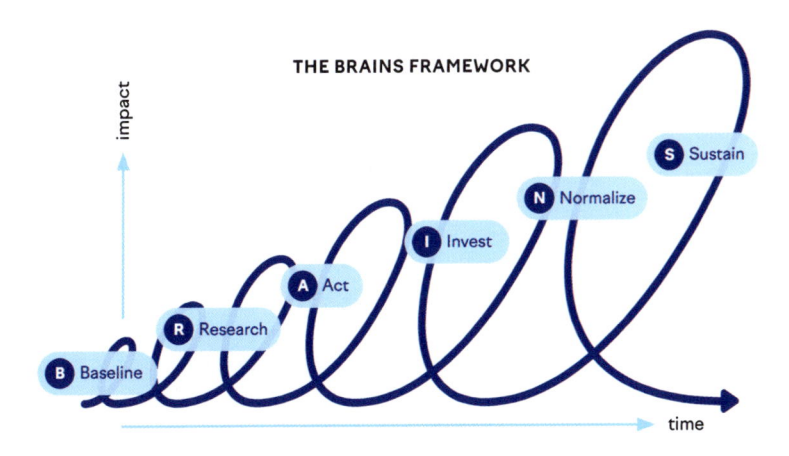

- **B** Baseline
- **R** Research
- **A** Act
- **I** Invest
- **N** Normalize
- **S** Sustain

(axes: impact vs. time)

tool that makes this easier. Again, this is a practice you'll be grateful for later.

Remember, the goal of this stage is not to create benchmarks for comparison between teams or individuals but rather to understand the present state so you can track improvement over time.

❷ RESEARCH

Knowing how your engineering teams experience their work is essential to achieving real engineering effectiveness wins.

Spend time shadowing engineers, conducting interviews, and doing hands-on work. Understand their daily challenges, frustrations, and moments of triumph. Pay particular attention to their work patterns, collaboration habits, and pain points. Watch for systemic issues that might be slowing them down or causing unnecessary stress. This first-hand understanding will be invaluable in identifying effective productivity and experiencing improvements.

Now is also the time to review your early Balance Framework data. Where are teams spending their time? Are there any surprises in the data? What adjustments need to be made?

❸ ACT

Now that you understand your engineers' current state and unique needs, it's time to tackle the quick wins. These are small, relatively easy improvements that nonetheless have a meaningful impact on the daily work of your teams. They could be anything from streamlining a standard process to eliminating a manual task or addressing a common source of frustration.

Who's going to work on these quick wins? For now, ensure that every one of your engineers knows they have permission to spend a little time making things better. Consider giving an engineer or two a few weeks on rotation to tackle an issue they're passionate about. Publicly celebrate both large and small improvements, and publicize the biggest opportunities.

❹ INVEST

With the low-hanging fruit addressed, it's time to focus on longer-term improvements at the organizational level. This often involves standardizing processes and tools across teams to reduce complexities and inconsistencies. Consider creating a dedicated platform team responsible for developing and maintaining shared tools and infrastructure. This investment in standardization can result in significant productivity boosts and make cross-team collaboration smoother and more effective.

Starting a team doesn't have to be a big production; the team lead already works at your company and is looking for a new opportunity. They're the self-directed, consistently high-impact person who's been poking at flaky tests and exceeded expectations last quarter by automating the entire build and deployment. They're a favorite collaborator among technical and non-technical folks alike, and they live for a good session of code archaeology.

The second engineer is also a colleague, and they were exceeding expectations within their first months. They're a smart execution machine in need of a good mentor. They're interested in humans and computers, hungry for challenging problems, and don't mind if people in the real world don't see their work.

> **Starting a team doesn't have to be a big production; the team lead already works at your company and is looking for a new opportunity.**

You will be most successful if this team thinks of internal engineer platforms as products and understands that products have users — users whom you need to talk to and listen to, especially when they're frustrated. A platform team's ultimate goal is to help those users produce more value for the same amount of effort.

❺ NORMALIZE

Standardization only delivers its full benefits when it becomes the default. You want to create happy paths for common development tasks, like adding a new API endpoint or building a new feature in the user interface. Drive the adoption of these new processes, making it the new normal for how things are done. This step will require clear communication to explain the changes and their benefits, thorough training to ensure everyone knows how to work within the new systems, and incentives to encourage adoption.

Support development teams throughout this transition and be open to feedback and suggestions for improvement. You can form an adoption squad to help teams make the transition and understand the benefits. Whenever possible, automate these transitions. When that's not possible, be sure to frame migration and usage instructions from the perspective of the platform user, not the platform creator.

6 SUSTAIN

Maintaining and improving engineering effectiveness is not a one-off task but a long-term commitment. As your company grows, so will the complexity of your engineering effectiveness challenges. Continually invest in improving your understanding of these evolving challenges and devising innovative solutions. Set strategic goals that reflect this commitment and foster a culture of continuous learning and improvement.

Remember, you are focusing on improving the overall effectiveness of your engineering organization, not on specific tactics or short-term goals. This mindset will help you remain adaptable and responsive to the changing needs of your engineering teams.

Managing change

Introducing new ways of working can be a daunting task. To do it well, you need to be thoroughly familiar with the change and its reasons while also considering the human ability to have big feelings about seemingly small changes. If you simply show up one day and say, "We're going to start measuring your work," things probably aren't going to go well.

Engineering leadership coach **Lara Hogan** writes and speaks about the *BICEPS framework*, developed by **Paloma Medina**, for understanding these human reactions. She emphasizes that everyone needs these six things to feel at ease about work and that any kind of change can suddenly disrupt any one of them.

Human need	Strategies
Belonging: The need to feel part of a community.	Ensure changes don't isolate individuals and maintain inclusive team dynamics.
Improvement/progress: The desire for personal and professional growth.	Link changes to development opportunities and career advancement.
Choice: The need for autonomy in work.	Involve employees in the change process and preserve their control over their work.
Equality/fairness: The importance of equitable treatment.	Apply changes consistently and transparently to avoid perceptions of unfairness.
Predictability: The preference for stability and certainty.	Communicate clearly about changes, providing a roadmap to alleviate anxiety.
Significance: The desire to do meaningful work.	Align changes with organizational goals and show how each role contributes to these objectives.

Putting It All Together

With these core needs in mind, it's easy to see that the first step in driving change is building trust with the people who will be affected. Trust, of course, has to be earned; even if you're operating in a generally high-trust environment, a change perceived as substantial can make people uneasy. Especially in low-trust environments, trust-building activities are going to be essential to successful change.

There are a few things you can do to earn trust around a change effort.

- Offer social proof that this change has been valuable elsewhere. Of course, all businesses are different, but if other businesses in your industry or at your stage have embraced certain practices, that should carry some weight.

- Run a pilot or proof of concept with a small set of teams. Iteration within a small group will help you decide what you want to roll out more widely.

- Participate in the process you're trying to improve and experience the difficulties first-hand. Share your learnings and let them inform your next steps.

- Celebrate successes widely and loudly, and incentivize the change you want to see.

Transparency likewise plays a huge role in how a change is received. Communicate clearly, frequently, and in multiple channels about why you're making the changes and what outcomes you hope to achieve from them. Communicate about what's working and what's not. Communicate about how leadership is contributing to and supporting the improvements in substantive ways.

Many organization-wide changes can take months to roll out, and rolling out an engineering effectiveness effort is no different. Along the way, inform your next steps with feedback from the people impacted by the changes you're making. As with any feedback, you don't have to act on all of it, but be prepared to explain how you choose what to act on and what to set aside.

> **Trust, of course, has to be earned; even if you're operating in a generally high-trust environment, a change perceived as substantial can make people uneasy.**

An engineering effectiveness effort can touch many of the BICEPS needs. For example, **belonging** can be affected if a person feels like their work won't be as valued when people start looking at effectiveness metrics, **predictability** can take a hit as software engineers wonder how their performance reviews will be affected, and **significance** can suffer if people feel their contribution is being reduced to numbers.

Whole books have been written on managing change, so we are, at best, scratching the surface with the concepts discussed here. The most important takeaway is that change is hard and thus needs to be approached with care. While you can just flip a switch to introduce a new process, tool, or other way of working, it's not likely to go well — a change of any significance needs thoughtful planning and communication.

What's next?

Throughout your effectiveness journey, it's important to focus on the ultimate goal: improving the experience and productivity of your engineers. This means avoiding getting too caught up in specific metrics or tactics at the expense of actual improvement.

This chapter provided a solid foundation for that journey, but once again, every organization and team is unique. Remember to remain flexible, responsive, adaptable, and cognizant of the changing needs of your engineering teams. ✹

FURTHER READING

Leading Change, by **John P. Kotter**. Kotter provides an eight-step process for leading change with powerful insights and practical tools.

The Goal: A Process of Ongoing Improvement, by **Eliyahu M. Goldratt**. This book introduces the Theory of Constraints, a methodology for identifying the most important limiting factor (i.e. bottleneck) in a process and systematically improving it.

Switch: How to Change Things When Change Is Hard, by **Chip Heath** and **Dan Heath**. Offers insights into how to effect transformative change in organizations, which is useful for understanding and managing the human side of organizational change.

Lean Thinking: Banish Waste and Create Wealth in Your Corporation, by **James P. Womack** and **Daniel T. Jones**. Provides a deep dive into lean principles, focusing on eliminating waste and improving efficiency, which are key to addressing process bottlenecks.

Crucial Conversations: Tools for Talking When Stakes Are High, by **Kerry Patterson**, **Joseph Grenny**, **Ron McMillan**, and **Al Switzler**. Valuable insights into handling high-stakes conversations.

Core Needs: BICEPS, by **Paloma Medina**. A framework for thinking about human needs, informed by neuropsychologists, psychologists, and sociologists. **palomamedina.com/biceps**

WE'RE HERE TO HELP

Now that you've made it this far, you understand that a lot goes into building and sustaining an effective engineering organization — more than technology, more than people, more than process.

When you're ready to introduce an engineering effectiveness program, this book will point you in the right direction. As you start to understand the landscape at your own company, consider the market for existing software that could support your particular goals.

Of your options, Swarmia is the only engineering effectiveness platform that focuses on holistic, continuous improvement across business outcomes, developer productivity, and developer experience.

If you want to increase healthy visibility into your engineering organization, have higher-quality conversations based on team-level productivity insights, and proactively improve the experience of building software at your company, let's talk. Swarmia just might be the right partner for your journey.

Whether you'd like a quick tour of Swarmia or a casual, no-strings-attached conversation with Otto or Rebecca, feel free to email us at **hello@swarmia.com**. ✸

About the authors

Rebecca Murphey is the Field CTO at Swarmia and hosts the Engineering Unblocked podcast. Previously, she drove engineering effectiveness efforts as an engineering leader at Stripe and Indeed, implementing some of the most transformative productivity improvements these companies saw during her tenure. She lives in Durham, North Carolina.

Otto Hilska is a serial entrepreneur and the founder and CEO of Swarmia. In 2009, he co-founded Flowdock (the Slack before Slack), acquired by Rally Software in 2013. After leaving Rally, Otto worked as the Chief Product Officer of Smartly.io, leading a fast-growing software organization while navigating emerging bottlenecks. He lives in Helsinki.

About Swarmia

We know from experience that building an effective software organization is not a one-and-done project. That's why we've designed Swarmia, the engineering effectiveness platform, to guide organizations on their continuous improvement journey, whether they're only just getting started or are further along the path.

Thousands of companies, from startups to enterprises, use Swarmia to maximize business outcomes, developer productivity, and developer experience. Learn more at swarmia.com. For more resources related to this book, visit swarmia.com/build.

Acknowledgments

Ari Koponen, for providing extensive technical editing and input.

Jack Humphrey, for providing invaluable feedback on an early draft of this book.

Eero Kettunen and **Miikka Holkeri**, for their input and feedback.

Pinja Dodik, for championing and guiding this project.

Feedback and errata

If you believe you've found an error in this book or something that can be improved, please contact books@swarmia.com to ensure your feedback is considered for the next edition.

Oskari Kallio in Helsinki designed the beautiful book you are holding, using Adobe InDesign like it's 2005. The typefaces used in this book are Factor A by **Ilya Naumoff** and Bagnard by **Sebastien Sanfilippo**. The book was printed by Amazon, edited by **Ari Koponen**, and copy-edited by **Christy Gibbs**.

Notes

Notes

Notes

Notes